Revise for GCSE PE: AQA/SEG

Kirk Bizley

To Stewart and Margaret

Heinemann Educational Publishers
Halley Court, Jordan Hill, Oxford OX2 8EJ
a division of Reed Educational & Professional Publishing Ltd

OXFORD   MELBOURNE   AUCKLAND
JOHANNESBURG   BLANTYRE   GABORONE
IBADAN   PORTSMOUTH (NH) USA   CHICAGO

Heinemann is a registered trademark of Reed Educational & Professional Publishing Ltd

First published 2000

04 03 02 01 00
9 8 7 6 5 4 3 2 1

British Library Cataloguing in Publication Data

A catalogue record for this book is available from the British Library

ISBN 0 435 10114 5

Typeset by Techtype, Abingdon
Printed and bound in Great Britain by The Bath Press, Bath

Acknowledgements

The publishers would like to thank the following for permission to reproduce copyright material:

The publishers have made every effort to contact copyright holders. However, if any material has been incorrectly acknowledged, the publishers would be pleased to correct this at the earliest opportunity

Cover photographs by: Gareth Boden (students playing basketball) and Sporting Pictures (speed skater/World Cup)

Tel: 01865 888058 www.heinemann.co.uk

Contents

How to use this book

This book has been written as a revision guide for students studying the GCSE Physical Education (and Physical Education /Games) AQA/SEG syllabuses. It can be used in conjunction with the following syllabuses as it completely matches the subject content:

- GCSE Physical Education: 2680
- GCSE Physical Education (Short Course): 1490
- GCSE Physical Education Games: 2685
- GCSE Physical Education: Games (Short Course) 1485

The section headings and syllabus references in this book refer to the full course examinations only. If you are taking the short course examinations (1490 and 1485), check the specific syllabus content. The short course is divided into two sections for theory work – Section A: Factors Affecting Performance and Section B: Factors Affecting Individual Participation. The sub-divisions of these two sections are also completely covered here but if you are a short course candidate, you will need to be selective about which sections you cover as you only have half of the theory content to cover compared to the full course candidates.

This book matches the content, sub-divisions and notes included in the syllabus. It contains only the basic information on the syllabus to ensure that you can answer any question set on any aspect of it. For more detailed coverage use *Examining Physical Education* AQA/SEG edition. This deals with the syllabus content, and issues raised by it, in more detail. You are also advised to keep up to date with current events, developments and changes which occur.

How each section is organized

Syllabus references
Each section starts with the relevant syllabus reference and follows the content in the same order as the syllabus.

Definitions
Definitions required in the syllabus are included under specific headings and match syllabus requirements.

Key points
These are designed to help you focus on the main issues raised in each section.

Hints and tips
These are pieces of extra guideline information which are designed to help you focus on the subject content of the syllabus and to make it more readily understandable, practical or clear.

Did You Know?
These back up pieces of information. They are a useful addition to your knowledge and can often be cited as examples in answers to questions.

Questions
The questions at the end of each section unit can all be answered using the information contained in the section. They also tend to summarize the notes in the syllabus details, so if you can answer them you should have sufficient knowledge to cover that particular section's requirements. You can either use the text when answering the questions, as examination practice – or answer without it.

Advice on the Exam Questions
This section contains useful tips and guidelines to help you prepare for the written exam. It makes general points about examination technique, as well as citing examples of questions with the correct strategy to answering them.

Section A: Health Related Fitness

1 Definitions of Health and Fitness

(a) Health

> **Definition**
> The World Health Organization has defined health as, 'a state of complete physical, mental and social well-being and not merely the absence of disease or infirmity. Health is one of the fundamental rights of every human being without distinction of race, religion, political belief, economics or social conditions.'

Influences on health

1. Use or abuse of alcohol, tobacco, medicines and drugs
2. Sex education – appropriate sexual behaviour
3. Family life education – especially caring for each other
4. Safety – in all environments: home, school, work, leisure activities
5. Health-related exercise – the maintenance of good health
6. Nutrition – a correct and balanced diet and preparation of food
7. Personal hygiene – cleanliness and avoiding disease
8. Environment – such as pollution, economic effects
9. Psychological aspects – mental health, emotional well-being and avoiding stress.

Key points

All the above are important but you should be aware of the particular effects of alcohol and smoking:

- alcohol – there can be immediate effects from too much alcohol, such as drunkenness which can cause vomiting and lack of co-ordination, as well as longer-term effects such as damage to internal organs (liver, muscle, heart) and body systems such as the digestive, immune and nervous
- smoking – the short-term effects may be vomiting but the long-term ones are the more dangerous, such as heart disease, lung cancer, chronic bronchitis, 'smoker's cough', sore throat, shortness of breath, breathing difficulties, headaches, dizziness and lack of concentration.

90 per cent of people in the UK drink alcohol.

> **QUESTION**
> How does being healthy and fit enable you to take part in sport more effectively?

(b) Physical Fitness

Definition

These are the factors which make up **physical fitness**:

- strength
- endurance
- body composition.
- speed
- flexibility

Key points

Fitness is a combination of factors. As well as **physical fitness** you may also need to consider **motor fitness** (see pages 8–9). There are two levels of fitness:

- **general fitness** – being in general good health and able to carry out everyday tasks comfortably (so is very closely linked with health – see page 5)
- **specific fitness** – this is a level beyond general fitness where you are able to meet the higher, more specific, demands of an activity or sport.

The following is a summary of the five factors in the definition above and their contribution to fitness.

Strength

Strength is a general term for applying a force against a resistance but there are different types of strength, used at different times, which have different definitions:

- **static strength** – the greatest amount of force which can be applied to an immovable object, for example, holding against the opposition in a rugby scrum
- **explosive strength** – muscular strength used in one short, sharp movement, for example, a sprinter leaving the blocks at the start of a 100-metre race
- **dynamic strength** – the muscular strength needed to support your own body weight over a prolonged period of time, for example, a gymnast on the pommel horse. Note that dynamic strength is very closely linked with endurance (see page 7) as the muscles need to keep working over quite a long period of time.

There are more than 600 muscles in your body.

Most activities require a combination of these three types of strength and in many activities you would use them all.

Speed

Speed is basically how fast you can move part, or the whole, of your body and is achieved through a combination of the following:

- **reaction time** – how quickly you can respond to something, for example, a sprinter reacting to the starting pistol sound
- **movement time** – how quickly you can carry out an actual movement, for example, the sprinter running down the track.

Speed in sport is measured in metres per second and a 60-metre sprint is the standard measure.

There are many factors which can affect an individual's speed, such as the proportion of fast twitch fibres in your muscles, your body shape and size, the duration of time or distance of the event/activity you are taking part in.

Endurance

Endurance is the ability to keep going with a movement or an activity for a relatively long period. There are two types of endurance:

- **muscular endurance** – the ability of muscles, or a group of muscles, to keep working against a resistance. The body needs to be able to avoid **muscular fatigue** which prevents you from being able to carry on
- **cardiovascular endurance** – the ability of the heart and lungs to keep supplying oxygen in the bloodstream to the body to provide the energy to sustain physical movement. This is why your heart and breathing rates both increase the longer you carry on with physical activity.

Often when you are taking part in an activity which requires endurance you will need a combination of both of these types. For example, a marathon runner requires muscular endurance in the leg muscles and cardiovascular endurance to supply enough oxygen to all of the working muscles during their 26 miles 385 yards race!

Flexibility

Flexibility is the range of movement around a joint. It is not just the ability to bend or stretch and it can only occur around a joint because bones and muscles must combine to allow movement at joints.

Body composition

Body composition is the amount of fat tissue which is present in the body. Height and weight are also factors but it is important not to have too high a level of excess fat in the body.

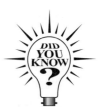

Another common term for endurance is stamina.

Flexibility is also often referred to as suppleness or mobility.

Approximately 60 per cent of your body weight is made up of water.

Hints and tips

Physical fitness is very much a combination of factors, which together make you generally fit. You would need to work quite hard on many (if not all) of the five factors if you aim to achieve specific fitness. Good health is needed as a starting point towards becoming fit.

FOCUS POINT

These are the tasks you should set yourself in order to answer questions in this area:

1. Tell the basic difference between general and specific fitness.

2. Give a basic definition of each of the five factors of physical fitness.

3. Give a basic example of the importance of each of the five factors as a component of physical fitness.

QUESTIONS

1. What would a performer need to concentrate on if they wanted to make themselves physically fit?
2. What factors combine to make one person physically fitter than another?
3. Choose one activity and describe how important each of the five factors of physical fitness are for that particular activity.

(c) Motor Fitness

> **Definition**
> These are the factors which make up **motor fitness**:
>
> - agility
> - power
> - balance
> - co-ordination.

 Key points

Remember that fitness is a combination of factors and that **motor fitness** is very closely linked with **physical fitness** (see pages 6–7).

Fitness is also relative to the demands made upon your body. For example, a club standard athlete would not have such a high level of fitness as an Olympic standard athlete. They would both train on particular aspects of fitness (both physical and motor) but the Olympic standard athlete would train much harder and longer.

The following is a summary of the four factors in the definition above and their contribution to fitness.

Agility

Agility is the combination of speed and co-ordination. If you are agile, you can change direction and your body position quickly – a soccer goalkeeper, for example, needs this to get into position to make saves.

Balance

Balance is being able to maintain your equilibrium, that is, being able to maintain your centre of gravity over a particular area of support. Standing and walking require balance but as you move your body into different positions you move your centre of gravity and therefore make balancing more difficult. Standing on one leg and then twisting sideways will move your centre of gravity and will straight away make balancing more difficult.

Maintaining good balance is very closely linked to two of the types of strength. You require **static** strength to hold a handstand steady and you need **dynamic** strength if you are a runner in motion.

Power

Power is the combination of the maximum amount of speed with the maximum amount of strength. The type of strength most closely linked with power is **explosive strength** because it is when using this type of strength that the most power is generated.

Power can only be used in short bursts because it is too tiring for a performer to keep using it for any long period.

Co-ordination

Co-ordination is the ability to properly control your body when performing a physical action. It requires being able to use all of your body systems together including the nervous system which sends the commands around the body. All physical activities require a great deal of co-ordination and the more difficult the skill, the greater the degree of co-ordination you need to perform it.

There is a test for agility known as the Illinois Agility Run.

It is very difficult to balance with your eyes shut. Close your eyes and balance on one leg. Make it more difficult by standing on a house brick. How long did you last?

Power generated by sports performers is measured in watts.

Co-ordination is affected by growth spurts – which explains why many teenagers experience a temporary decrease in their levels of co-ordination.

Hints and tips

Fitness should be considered as a general term and when answering questions about it you should think about all the factors which make it up unless you have been asked to consider any one in particular.

Most of the factors of fitness above can be affected, or even changed, by regular training in order to improve them (see pages 56–8). There are also other things which can affect your fitness levels. These include:

- **age** – generally speaking, fitness levels decrease with age after reaching adulthood
- **gender** – on average women only have two-thirds of the strength of men, a higher percentage of fat, a broader, flatter pelvis, faster maturity rates and greater flexibility (due to less muscle mass)
- **somatotype** – see page 64.

You do not really have any control over these factors and individual differences have to be taken into consideration when you consider the fitness levels which someone may be able to attain.

There are also some additional factors that can have either a temporary or permanent effect on fitness levels:

- **physical disability** – this can range from the less severe, such as sight difficulties right through to paralysis that necessitates the use of a wheelchair
- **illness, injury or medical condition** – a broken arm or leg, a cold or conditions such as asthma or hay fever can all be important
- **diet** – see pages 10–13
- **drugs, smoking or alcohol** – see page 5
- **weight and height**
- **psychological factors** – such as stress and anxiety, see pages 68–9

QUESTIONS

Some of these questions refer to motor fitness in particular and some to fitness in general.

1 What are the **four** factors which combine to make up motor fitness?
2 Choose **one** activity and describe how important each of the **four** factors of motor fitness are for that particular activity.
3 Choose **one** activity and describe how factors you have no control over may affect your levels of fitness.
4 Describe some factors which could have a temporary effect on your fitness levels.
5 Which factors of fitness could be improved through regular training?

What are the differences in the levels of fitness required for a high standard performer compared to someone who is competing at a basic, lower level?

2 Diet

(a) For the Maintenance of Good Health

Definition
A balanced diet is the correct intake of all of the appropriate amounts of nutrients which provides the body with energy.

 Key points

Food is the main energy source of the body and we cannot survive without it. The body requires the following in order to function properly:

- carbohydrates
- fats
- proteins
- vitamins
- minerals
- water
- fibre.

Carbohydrates

These are divided into two groups:

- **simple carbohydrates** (sugars) – including glucose, sucrose, fructose and lactose
- **complex carbohydrates** (starches) – these are contained in bread, pasta, rice, potatoes and pulses.

Carbohydrates are the main energy providers and if, when taken in, they are not needed immediately, they are stored as **glycogen** in the liver and muscles.

A balanced diet contains approximately 55 per cent carbohydrates.

Fats

Fat contains substances called **fatty acids** and there are three main types:

- **saturates** (saturated fatty acids) – are found in meat, meat fats and dairy products
- **monounsaturates** (monounsaturated fatty acids) – found in olive oil
- **polyunsaturates** (polyunsaturated fatty acids) – found in margarines and oils made from seeds and nuts such as sunflower, soya and corn.

Most fats contain a mixture of these fatty acids and they are important because:

- fats provide a concentrated energy source
- fats stored under the skin help keep the body warm
- fat stored around the heart has a protective effect
- foods with a high fat content also contain fat soluble vitamins
- essential fatty acids cannot be made in the body and must therefore be provided by food.

A balanced diet contains approximately 30 per cent fat.

Proteins

Proteins are made from building blocks called **amino acids**. The body needs twenty different amino acids to make all the proteins necessary for good health.

Proteins are found in animal sources, such as meat, fish, eggs, milk and cheese. These contain all of the essential amino acids. Other sources, such as beans, lentils, cereals, bread, pasta and rice, lack one or more of the essential amino acids.

A balanced diet contains approximately 15 per cent protein.

Proteins are needed in the diet:

- for the formation, growth and repair of tissues, e.g. muscle, hair and skin
- to make enzymes and hormones.

If you are physically active you need a good supply of proteins. You need slightly more if you train hard or for long periods.

Vitamins

For this examination you need to know about vitamins A, C and D only.

You only need vitamins in small amounts but they are essential for good health. They are divided into two groups:

- **fat soluble** (vitamins A and D) – can be stored in the body
- **water soluble** (vitamin C) – cannot be stored so you need a constant daily supply.

Vitamins are needed to:

- protect the body and maintain the body chemistry
- enable growth and maintenance of bones, teeth, skin and glands
- help with digestion
- help with the stability of the nervous system
- help tissue growth
- increase resistance to bacteria and disease.

As each different vitamin was discovered it was given a letter.

These are the facts about the three vitamins you need to know:

- **vitamin A** – mainly found in milk, butter, eggs, oily fish, cod or halibut liver oil, spinach and cabbage. Necessary for keeping skin and bone healthy, preventing infection of the nose and throat and helping with good vision
- **vitamin C** – mainly found in fresh vegetables and fruit, especially citrus fruits such as oranges. Necessary for helping heal wounds, keeping gums and teeth healthy and protecting against colds. A deficiency in this vitamin can cause **scurvy**
- **vitamin D** – mainly found in oily fish and fish oils, eggs, butter (and can be absorbed through sunlight!). Necessary to help build up bones and teeth. A deficiency can cause **rickets** – poorly developed 'soft' bones.

Minerals

For this examination you only need to know about **iodine**, **iron** *and* **calcium**.

Some minerals are only required in small amounts and these are known as trace elements. You take in minerals through eating vegetables and meats and they are important because they:

- help to build tissues
- are the main constituents of bones and teeth
- help to release and use energy in the body
- provide soluble salts in the body fluids
- help with the correct functioning of cells and muscles.

A deficiency in minerals can cause stunted growth, damaged eyesight and weak, malformed bones.

These are the facts about the minerals you need to know:

- **iodine** – mainly found in dairy products, seafood and drinking water. It maintains the health of the thyroid gland which makes hormones

- **iron** – mainly found in liver, meat, egg yolk, whole grain or enriched breads and cereals and green vegetables. It helps produce haemoglobin in the red blood cells and therefore helps deliver oxygen to the body tissues to provide energy
- **calcium** – mainly found in milk and milk products, salmon, sardines, beans, broccoli and green vegetables. It helps harden bones and teeth, muscle contraction and clotting of the blood.

Most people take in sufficient minerals in their normal balanced diet. You may need slightly more of some minerals if you are exercising or training regularly.

Water

Water is the most important daily dietary intake because a lack of it can cause illness, or even death, quicker than the lack of any other substance. Water is lost naturally through urine, sweat, expired air and faeces. The absence, or rapid loss, of water is known as **dehydration**. This is a serious condition and one which sports performers should be aware of.

When you are exercising more water is lost from the body than when at rest. Some of this is through sweating and also through water vapour when breathing out. The amount of water you lose when exercising depends on the intensity of the exercise, the duration of the exercise and the temperature and humidity of the surroundings. It is very important to replace water when you are exercising, especially in hot conditions, or if you are exercising for a long time.

Fibre

The main function of fibre is to keep the digestive system healthy. It helps to prevent constipation and can reduce the chances of getting bowel cancer. Fibre can be taken in through wholemeal bread and pasta, wholegrain cereals, brown rice, pulses, fruits, vegetables, nuts and seeds.

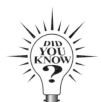

On average your body loses about two and a half litres of water every day!

> ### Hints and tips
> You should be aware that people need to have a balanced diet and know which nutrients make up one. You should be able to outline briefly what all of the essential nutrients are, what they consist of and the types of food which are rich in them.

The recommended daily intake of dietary fibre is 18 grammes a day.

Energy equation and basal metabolic rate

Even when you are resting, energy is being used by your body. The **energy equation** means that you should take in the required amount of energy (through a balanced diet) to equal the amount of energy you use through the activity you do.

Basal metabolic rate is the amount of energy needed for important processes like breathing and keeping the heart beating. This can vary between individuals.

If you have an unbalanced energy equation it can mean that your diet is providing more energy than is needed. The extra will be stored as **adipose tissue** (or fat) and you will gain weight. If this goes on for some time then you may become extremely overweight or **obese**. The reverse effect can occur when you do not take in enough energy. This result in extreme weight loss can cause **malnutrition** or **anorexia**, which is a refusal to eat.

The **energy value** of food depends upon the combined amount of energy provided by each of the nutrients. This is expressed in kilojoules (kJ) or kilocalories (kcal). In everyday terms it is referred to as **calories**.

Foods can be divided up into four main groups, with a smaller fifth group:

1 bread, other cereals and potatoes
2 fruit and vegetables
3 milk and dairy products
4 meat, fish and alternatives
5 (fatty and sugary foods).

 FOCUS POINT Copy out the following table. Use the information from this unit to complete it.

Dietary substances	Foods they are found in	Reasons they are required
carbohydrates		
fats		
proteins		
vitamins		
minerals		
water		
fibre		

Remember that the table above requires information about a healthy diet and not any specific, more detailed responses about particular diets. These are considered on pages 10–12.

Nutrition is the process of receiving food.

QUESTIONS

1 Name all the nutrients which together make up a balanced diet.
2 What are the **two** carbohydrate groups? Give both the terms for them.
3 Name the **three** main types of fats. Why do you need fats in a balanced diet?
4 What are proteins made from? Name **two** things they are needed for.
5 What are the **two** groups of vitamins?
6 For each of the following, name some foods rich in this vitamin and describe why they are vital in a balanced diet.
   a vitamin A   **b** vitamin C   **c** vitamin D
7 Which vitamin deficiencies can lead to scurvy and to rickets?
8 Name **four** things which minerals can provide.
9 For the following minerals, describe the foods they may be found in and their main health function: **a** iodine   **b** iron   **c** calcium
10 Why is fibre needed in a balanced diet?
11 What problem can arise through a lack of, or shortage of, water?
12 What do the energy equation and basal metabolic rate mean?

(b) Specific Requirements for Performers

 Key points

Everyone needs to follow a balanced diet but sports performers must consider their diet very carefully. The following are the specific factors which you need to take into account:

- **age of performer**
- **type of activity undertaken.**

Age

Younger people, especially those who are undergoing a growth spurt, may need a greater amount of food to enable their bodies to cope with the demands put on them.

The general rule is that as we get older, the demand for food tends to decrease and that we need to regulate our food intake and weight more carefully.

Amounts and types of activity undertaken

Different activities have different demands and dietary requirements as these examples show:

- **gymnasts** – need to remain fairly small and light. They should avoid too many fatty foods which could lead to an increase in body weight. They do need plenty of strength and energy so require a good balance of carbohydrates, proteins and fats
- **hockey players (and other invasion game players)** – do not need to be either particularly light or heavy but they require energy to be able to keep going in matches and training. Their diet should be fairly normal but with sufficient carbohydrates, proteins and fats to supply their energy needs
- **weightlifters** – need to have a great deal of body weight and may even have to increase it deliberately to get into a certain body weight category. They may try to increase their **bulk** so the quantities they eat may be increased with carbohydrates and fats as a priority. To increase strength they may add extra proteins which help muscle development.

 Key points

When discussing and considering diet, remember:

- the quantities of food consumed are always as important as the types of food
- dietary needs will vary at particular times as shown below.

Before activity

There should always be a period of preparation for performers and diet is an important factor. They may need to be particularly light (or even heavy). This has to be planned out over quite a long period of time.

Men need to consume about 3,000 kcal a day (for women it is 2,200). This needs to be doubled if you are particularly active or train regularly.

Top performers often adjust their diet for up to a week before an important event. A good example of this are marathon runners who decrease the amount of carbohydrates at the start of this period and then increase it just before the event. This is known as **carbohydrate loading**.

You should never eat too close to training or taking part in exercise. A general rule is to wait at least two hours so that the body is not coping with digesting food and meeting the demands of increased exercise levels. It is all right to take liquids just before without causing problems.

During activity

No food should be eaten during an activity because it puts a strain on the body. (Small amounts are all right, i.e. parts of fruits such as bananas.) It is important during exercise to take in fluids and drinks in order to avoid **dehydration**. Many performers take energy supplement drinks.

After activity

After strenuous activity it is important to replace all the energy which has been used up. However, this should not be done immediately!

You probably won't feel like eating anyway because exercise can be an appetite suppressant. You can take liquids immediately but you should leave the same two-hour gap before eating any substantial amounts of food. Then you should get back to the established pattern of preparation as before.

Extreme stomach cramps and pain can be felt if you eat too much either just before, or just after, exercising hard.

 Key points

- You must be able to link the information you have about nutrients and a balanced diet and apply it to the specific requirements of particular performers.
- It is often easier to consider two extremes if asked to compare different performers. So the gymnast and weightlifter examples above would be good ones to use.
- The importance, and need for liquids is a very important factor.

QUESTIONS

1 Compare **two** different performers in two different activities and describe the dietary requirements of each.

2 If you were the trainer of a marathon runner, what sort of dietary needs would you suggest in the following three stages:

   a in the long-term period building up to a race
   b during the race
   c the period immediately after the race?

3 Why is it important for sports performers to maintain fluid levels?

3 Exercise

(a) For the Maintenance of Good Health

Definition
A basic, common definition of exercise is 'healthy physical exertion'.

 Key points

Exercise can be considered to take place on two levels:

- the basic level where it is used to maintain good health. It is therefore closely linked with health (see page 5) and is very similar to the levels required for general fitness
- the higher level for performers needing to achieve targets in their sport (see pages 18–19).

The following is a summary of the basic points.

Benefits of exercise

The amount of exercise you do needs to match your energy requirements (see page 12) in order to control weight. However, there are other benefits to exercise:

- it improves body shape
- it releases tension and stress (also known as psychological benefits) which can add to the enjoyment of life
- it reduces the chances of getting illnesses and disease
- it provides a physical challenge to aim for
- it helps maintain a good level of fitness
- it tones up the body and the muscles, leading to an improvement in **posture**. This helps prevent curvature of the back, strained back and abdominal muscles and rounded shoulders, impairing breathing
- it increases the basic levels of strength and stamina, for example, being able to carry out manual tasks repeatedly, such as stacking shelves, standing on your feet all day
- it increases basic levels of flexibility, for example, tying up your shoelaces or reaching up for a book
- it provides social benefits – such as meeting new friends with shared common interests.

 Key points

Having established the need for, and benefits of exercise, it is also important to be able to say what amount and type of exercise is most suitable. This depends on:

- age
- gender
- activity level.

The following guidelines will help you with this.

You must exercise your body to some degree daily or your muscles can literally waste away. This is known as atrophy.

A job which involves sitting down for most of the time with little or no movement or exercise is known as sedentary.

Physical condition

If someone is not very healthy or has not been exercising regularly, they may need to see their doctor for advice on how much they should exercise. This is particularly sensible if the person is middle-aged or older and has not been exercising regularly before.

Many people are now being 'prescribed' exercise by their doctors who have arrangements with local leisure centres to help and advise patients with their exercise.

Long-term aims

Exercise has to be done regularly to achieve any benefits and it should be increased gradually. Exercising for about 15–20 minutes 4 or 5 times a week is a good guideline. You should also make sure that you do not overdo it – getting to the point of being pleasantly tired is enough. Good all-round exercise such as swimming is best. Joining some sort of club might help to make sure that the exercise is regularly done.

The minimum exercise for good health

The following suggested forms of exercise are quite basic but may be all that is needed to maintain good heath:

- Don't be driven everywhere but walk short distances instead.
- Try to walk at least part of a journey; if you travel by bus get off one stop early.
- Use a bicycle for transport.
- Walk up stairs (or some of them) instead of using escalators.
- Get used to doing some basic stretching or flexibility exercises every day.

Just being slightly short of breath is not a sign of exercising too much but if you are too short of breath to even talk properly you have overdone it!

 **Key points**

Exercise should make you fitter in the long term but it also has some immediate effects:

- the rate of breathing and the heart beat (pulse rate) increase
- body temperature increases and sweat appears on the skin surface
- skin may appear to redden, especially on the face
- there may be a feeling of tiredness or 'heaviness' in some muscles.

QUESTIONS

1 Describe some of the main benefits of exercising regularly.
2 What guidelines should someone consider when they are planning to start exercising?
3 Are there cases where a person would be advised not to exercise?
4 Why do doctors 'prescribe' exercise to some of their patients?
5 What special considerations should someone who has a sedentary job take into account when planning a basic exercise programme?
6 What are the main short-term effects that exercising can have on the body?

(b) For the Performer

Key points

General exercise guidelines apply to all people, which is why they are an important factor in maintaining good health. Guidelines for exercise become more specialized when they are applied to sports performers who require a higher level of exercise. They would be targeting the factor of improving their fitness as the main reason for exercising.

The following factors are specific to performers.

Specific requirements

Different activities require different amounts of exercise. These may be actual physical requirements, such as certain aspects or components of fitness, and the importance of both general and specific fitness have to be taken into account.

Some activities have certain playing seasons and rest periods known as the 'closed season', when players recuperate. (For instance, cricket is a summer activity in the UK and the 'closed season' is during the winter months.) This resting period is often a time when the performers train, especially for any type of endurance event where there is a long build-up to get ready for competition.

As any playing season approaches training is usually stepped up because the performer will aim to 'peak' at a particular time, depending on the game or event being planned.

If the performers are taking part in team events, they will get together as a team just before the start of the season to practise skills and any 'set plays' which they may need to use.

Many performers need to train all the year round and they will often temporarily move abroad during the UK winter because it is not possible for them to train properly in the cold climate. This really only applies to professional athletes because of the cost involved.

Many performers play their particular sport abroad whenever it is the season in that particular country. For example, many professional cricketers play for English clubs during the UK summer and then play in Australia, New Zealand or South Africa during their summer.

A sprint athlete may train all year round and focus their training to peak for one particular race – which they hope is going to take about nine and half seconds!

American football has one of the shortest playing seasons as it only lasts for about four months of the year.

FOCUS POINT
Fill in the table on the next page, which is linked to the different types of physical activity available in the practical component. Choose one particular activity from the group heading. State what the season and closed playing seasons are (or if they do not apply to that particular activity), as well as the types of training which should be covered during the closed season.

Practical activity	Playing season/ Closed season	Closed season exercise training
Group 1 Invasion game		
Group 1 Net/wall game		
Group 1 Striking/Fielding/Target		
Group 2 Gymnastic activity		
Group 3 Dance		
Group 4 Athletic activity		
Group 5 Swimming		

QUESTIONS

1 Why do higher level sports performers have to consider and plan more specifically for their exercise levels than people who only have to consider exercise for the maintenance of good health?

2 What do you understand by the terms 'playing season' and 'closed season'?

3 What is meant by performers 'peaking' and what steps would they take in order to achieve this? Give an example of when and how this might happen.

4 How and why would the climate affect a performer's preparation for their game or event?

4 Hygiene and Safety

(a) Personal Hygiene

Definition
Personal hygiene includes all of the following:

- washing
- prevention of disease
- good food preparation practices
- clothing
- social considerations.

- cleaning
- prevention of infection
- dental care
- self-esteem and confidence

 Key points

Personal hygiene is very closely linked with good health. Failing to have good personal hygiene habits could lead to your becoming unhealthy. This in turn will affect your ability to perform well in physical activity.

To answer questions on personal hygiene you need to have information on the following:

- the need for regular showering/washing
- wearing correct and appropriate clothing
- proper care of the feet
- problems caused by wearing incorrectly fitting footwear.

Hints and tips
Areas of hygiene tend to overlap so information on the aspects listed in the Key points above comes under several of the headings below. For instance, proper care of the feet is covered in both 'Showering/washing' and 'Cleaning and correct clothing', as well as specifically in 'Correct footwear'.

Your skin is the largest organ in your body. On an adult male it can be about 3 square metres in area!

The following is the summary of the basic points you need to know.

Showering/washing
This has to be done regularly. You might do something like washing your hands several times a day but you should also make sure that you wash all of your body and skin regularly.

Lack of washing can cause:

- **skin diseases** – infection is introduced by germs building up on the body or getting in cuts or sores
- **body odours** – if sweat is not removed by washing it smells unpleasant. You can also use anti-perspirants/deodorants to prevent this unpleasant smell. They can reduce the effect of the sweating as well.

Not drying properly after washing can also cause problems such as:

- **athlete's foot** – this is a fungal infection which causes itching and splitting skin between and underneath the toes. This can be prevented by drying the area around the toes properly after washing. If the infection sets in then you have to use special powders and creams to treat it.

Cleaning and correct clothing

Everything you use should be clean. This also applies to your clothing and to sports clothing in particular.

You should have a set of clothing specially for sporting activities and this should be changed and washed regularly as it quickly becomes both dirty and sweaty. Underwear and socks should also be changed regularly – you should never wear the same item of underwear before, during and after taking part in physical activity!

Clothing has to be appropriate to an activity. Here are some examples:

- loose-fitting clothing in team games enables you to move more easily and comfortably
- tight-fitting clothing is more appropriate in a gymnastic activity such as trampolining or vaulting.

Remember, too, that long hair should *always* be tied back for both hygiene and safety reasons.

Correct footwear

Footwear must always be appropriate to an activity and has to fit correctly, otherwise the following problems might occur:

- **blisters** – caused by the foot rubbing against the footwear. Not wearing socks could be the cause, but it is more likely that footwear is too tight
- **corns** – hardened and painful skin on the feet, usually on the sides. These can also be caused by wearing footwear which is too tight
- **bunions** – inflamed joints, usually on the big toe; made far worse if footwear is too tight
- **verrucas** – a form of wart on the foot which can be passed on by sharing footwear. Made more painful with tight footwear.

QUESTIONS

1 Why should you always shower or bath immediately following physical activity?
2 Name an infection that can occur on the feet, explaining how it may be caused.
3 Why is it important to tie back long hair when trampolining?
4 Explain what the following are and how they are caused.

    a blisters   **c** bunions
    b corns   **d** verrucas

(b) Prevention of Injury
(i) Reasons for Warm-ups/Warm-downs

 Key points

A warm-up is something which should be performed each time before you take part in physical activity. At the end of each session you should finish with a warm-down (also often referred to as a 'cool-down').

This is primarily for safety reasons – to prevent injury.

Warm-ups

You should always complete a warm-up because:

An international standard gymnast would expect to warm up for at least an hour before doing an event in a competition.

- it increases the body temperature – this has the effect of actually 'warming up' the muscles. This makes them more responsive and able to contract and relax more effectively
- it increases your range of movement – the blood flow through the muscles is increased and this improves their ability to contract quickly. The muscle fibres and tendons are better prepared to allow you a full range of movement
- movement skills can be practised. These can be done through the full range of movement you might need to use when taking part
- it allows you to increase gradually the amount of effort you are putting in up to the full pace you will need
- it can act as a form of psychological preparation to get you mentally ready to take part.

The warm-up itself usually consists of different stages or phases. The routine should contain specific types of exercises:

- **a continuous movement activity** – these are sometimes also referred to as 'pulse raisers'. The idea of this is to increase the heart rate and the body temperature so that the blood flow to the muscles is increased. You must be careful not to overdo this part of the warm-up so that you don't tire yourself out
- **light exercises** – these should specifically work the major muscle groups to be used such as press-ups for the arms, or sit-ups for the abdominals. These also should not be overdone to tire out the muscles but just to warm them up
- **flexibility exercises** – these should concentrate on all areas of the body. All the major joints should be stretched and exercised. A little extra stretching and mobility work would benefit any particular body area which is going to be used a lot. For example, any activity requiring running would definitely need plenty of stretching and mobility of the hamstring area.

At all international athletics events the organizers provide a 'warm-up track' where the competitors can prepare for their race.

The amount of time you spend on the warm-up, and the stages will vary on the type of activity you are preparing for. Just a few minutes may be enough for some performers while others might need longer. You may also need to warm up several times before performing. Many substitutes in team games have to do this several times before they actually get to join in the game.

Warm-down

This is often referred to as the 'cool-down' and it is just as essential as the warm-up in any exercise session. Just stopping immediately after you have finished exercising is not a good idea and you can gain many benefits from your warm-down, for example:

- it allows the body to recover – you can return the body back to its pre-exercise state gently, just as you built it up in your warm-up
- it helps to remove waste products such as lactic acid which are dispersed more quickly with an increased blood flow. This reduces the chances of muscle soreness and injury
- it helps prevent blood pooling. If you stop suddenly the blood returning to the heart drops quite dramatically which can make you feel dizzy and light-headed. The warm-down enables the blood flow to be maintained
- the muscles are allowed to return to their normal temperature slowly. Quickly cooling them can result in muscle damage – this is why it is a good idea to perform some flexibility/mobility exercises at this stage because the muscles are nicely stretched and pliable allowing you a full range of movement
- it allows you to both mentally and physically relax.

One of the best ways to warm down is to repeat what you did for your warm-up with a greatly reduced number of exercises – in this case the warm-down becomes a shortened version of your warm-up.

Key point

A warm-down is something which should be carried out at the end of each training/exercise session. Its main purpose is the prevention of injury.

QUESTIONS

1 Give **five** reasons why you should always complete a warm-up before exercising.

2 Describe the **three** phases, or stages, of a warm-up. For each of these stages describe why there is a need to include it and what benefits it has.

3 How much time would you expect to spend on a warm-up? Would it vary with different types of activities and if so, how?

4 Give some actual examples of what you would include in a warm-up. Explain each in detail and also explain what it is going to achieve.

5 Give **five** reasons why you should always finish with a warm-down.

6 Explain briefly what you should include in a warm-down session.

(ii) Correct Actions, Clothing, Footwear to Prevent Injury

Key points

Injury to yourself and other players can be prevented in a variety of ways including:

- the use of correct actions (i.e. performing sporting activities using the correct technique, such as tackling properly in rugby)
- wearing the correct and appropriate clothing
- wearing the correct and appropriate footwear.

Correct actions

In all activities using the correct technique when performing movements and actions usually means that you are doing it as safely as possible. The following are some examples from each of the activity groups:

- **Group 1** – use of the correct tackling technique – for example, in rugby, soccer or hockey avoids injury to yourself or other players
- **Group 2** – using incorrect technique in any of the movements such as rotation on the trampoline, or when vaulting, can be dangerous. Movements where a landing is involved also require the correct technique
- **Group 3** – whilst dance does not have set movements as such, there is a need for 'locomotion, jumping and turning' which all require the correct technique
- **Group 4** – all the athletic throwing events such as the discus, shot and javelin need the use of proper technique if the direction of the throw is to be correct and therefore safe
- **Group 5** – incorrect diving technique can be dangerous. Using the wrong treading water technique can also cause problems.

One general point you should remember about correct actions concerns lifting and lowering any sports equipment. A good example of this is when putting out a trampoline as the 'wings' need to be correctly pulled out. Also the rule of 'keeping a straight back and bending the legs' when lifting and carrying should always be considered.

Statistically, the most dangerous sport in the world is golf. More people die playing it than any other sport – however, this is not due to the dangerous nature of the game but more to the age of the players who die of natural causes when playing!

Hints and tips

If you have a question in the exam about safety and sporting activities, try to choose an example from an activity which gives you the best opportunity to answer the question easily and fully. In the list above, the examples from Groups 1 and 2 are probably best.

Correct clothing

Most sporting activities have specific clothing and certain activities have special protective clothing as well, particularly games activities such as:

- **hockey** – goalkeepers wear full protective clothing. This includes full face mask, leg pads, chest pad and 'kickers' for the feet
- **soccer** – players wear shin pads (often with built in ankle protectors). Some goalkeepers wear slightly padded shirts (to absorb some of the impact when landing, especially on the shoulders) as well as gloves
- **rugby** – pack members wear scrum caps to protect their ears. Many players also wear shoulder pads and chest pads to make tackling, and being tackled, safer
- **cricket** – batters wear a variety of protective clothing against being hit by the ball. Close fielders wear helmets and shin pads.

There are also some general rules about clothing:

- For some activities clothing needs to be loose and not too tight-fitting in order to prevent rubbing (possible blisters), or chafing (tight shorts or coarse material shorts will cause this). This is also for comfort.
- In other activities, clothing needs to be tight and close-fitting. In trampoline activities, for example, loose clothing could get caught in the springs or the bed.

Correct footwear

Sports shoes are important because they give support to the arches and cushion the ankles. Also shoes that are too high at the back can damage the Achilles' tendon. The footwear you wear should be very specific to the activity you are taking part in. Most sports/activities have their own specialist footwear which is widely known. The most common and obvious examples are:

- **studded boots** – worn in games played on grass (i.e. soccer, rugby and hockey) to give the correct grip
- **moulded stud footwear** – for artificial surfaces such as astro-turf
- **running spike shoes** – for both grass tracks and artificial track surfaces
- **light 'slipper' type shoes** – for gymnastics and trampoline work to protect toes but allow free movement.

QUESTIONS

1 Choose an activity and give an example where using a correct action could help to prevent an injury.

2 What are the basic rules for lifting, carrying and lowering sports equipment which you should always consider?

3 Give an example from a sporting activity where a player should wear specific protective clothing and describe how it can prevent injury.

4 Explain why it might be correct to wear loose-fitting clothing for one activity and tight-fitting for another.

5 Describe the correct type of footwear which should be worn for a particular sport and explain why it is appropriate for that activity.

(iii) Safety in Relation to Health and Others

Key points

This section refers to safety in general and, specifically, to how taking part safely can prevent injury. There are various safety rules which apply in all activities and situations, but there are also ones which are specific to a particular activity.

General safety

Safety considerations come under four headings covering the general rules which you should observe:

- **Preparation** – you must get yourself properly prepared to take part in any form of physical activity. This includes:

  1 *Training*: you need to get yourself in physical shape to take part. (How would you possibly take part in a marathon if you did not train before it?) You must also become familiar with the game/activity, i.e. learn the basic rules/regulations. (Not knowing the rules about tackling in rugby, for example, could put you in a dangerous situation in a game!)
  2 *Warm-up*: see page 22. This is essential as a safety precaution before any activity
  3 *Physical state*: you should always remove all jewellery such as watches, earrings and bracelets. In netball the length of your fingernails is checked by the umpire. This includes making sure that you are wearing any protective items such as gum shields or special protective padding items (see page 25).

- **Participation** – whenever you take part you need to be aware of the following:

  1 *Fair play*: you must not play dangerously or recklessly and you must always stick to the rules of an activity – particularly where physical contact is allowed. (It can be just as dangerous playing on a squash court as on a rugby pitch if you are not aware of the rules!)
  2 *Officials*: these are there to make sure the game is played correctly and players must obey their instructions.

- **Equipment** – this is one of the most important factors and in all cases the following must be considered:

  1 *Correctness*: the right equipment must be worn or used at the correct time and it must be appropriate to the activity. It also has to be worn correctly, so straps or buckles have to be done up. It must fit properly – a badly-fitting gum shield, for example, could be fatal! The equipment must only be used for protection and not as any form of weapon or dangerous object.
  2 *Condition*: all equipment must be checked regularly and kept in good order. Wood can splinter or chip, metal can corrode and rust and some materials can rot. (A damaged hockey stick could split when hitting the ball and flying splinters could cause injury to several players.)

- **Environment** – this is not always something which a player has control over but it must be considered in two ways:

  1 *Uncontrolled environment*: this includes such things as weather conditions. The ground condition, and therefore the playing conditions, can be affected by the weather. The ground can be wet, slippery, too dry and therefore hard, frozen and dangerous, and even flooded. Pursuing an outdoor activity in severe weather could be extremely dangerous and such conditions could even stop a game when it is underway. If there is an electrical storm and lightning then games should be held up until they pass.

  2 *Controlled environment*: these are things which you *can* do something about. A pitch can be inspected before a match to check for broken glass, stones or other objects. Arrangements can be made for crowds or spectators to make sure that they are safe from the players and the players are also safe from them.

Specific activity group examples

These are examples from each of the activity groups of factors which relate specifically to safety:

- **Group 1** – *invasion/striking games*: use of shin pads, face mask/helmet, gum shield, batting/goalkeeper's gloves, etc.; *net/wall games*: goggles, secure net/posts, clear playing area
- **Group 2** – *gymnastics*: condition of mats, qualified staff/spotters, overhanging beams, use of magnesium carbonate (put on the hands to improve grip), use of spotters when weight training, removal of jewellery, etc.; lifting, carrying and placing equipment safely
- **Group 3** – *dance*: condition of floor mats, warm-up, removal of jewellery, use of appropriate clothing, etc.
- **Group 4** – *athletics*: use of landing areas for high jump and pole vault; rake being removed from pit (*long jump/triple jump*); not throwing until told to do so (*throwing events*); not running to collect javelins, etc.
- **Group 5** – *swimming*: not running on the pool side, checking the depth of water, not jumping in; not going out of one's depth, etc.

QUESTIONS

1 Explain **two** general safety rules which would apply in all cases of taking part in a physical activity.

2 Choose **one** activity and explain the various safety measures you would take into consideration before you took part.

3 What are the different ways you can prepare yourself to be able to take part more safely in a physical activity?

4 Describe some of the injuries which could occur if you did not take the appropriate safety precautions.

(c) First Aid

 Key points

You only need a fairly basic knowledge of first aid and specifically that which is connected with taking part in physical activities. In most cases this is a knowledge of the type of injuries which can occur. You are advised not to try to give first aid treatment using any of this knowledge.

Common injuries

The following are the injuries which you need to know about. For each there is a description of what it is, what could cause it and what action should be taken.

Joint and muscle injuries

- **strains** – these are caused by overstretching of a muscle and they can also be caused by a twist or a wrench. They may be referred to as a 'pulled muscle'. They are quite painful and there may be some reduced or weakened movement where the injury has occurred. Bandaging the area will help to give some support and elastic bandages are particularly good for this
- **sprains** – these occur where there is overstretching, or tearing, of ligaments at a joint. They are most often caused by a sudden wrench or twist and it is a very common injury to the ankle joint. A sprain is more serious than a strain. It can be difficult to tell it from a break or a dislocation so it should always be treated in the same way as a fracture. It would need to be X-rayed and treated by a doctor
- **tendon and ligament damage** – tendons attach the muscles to the bones and ligaments attach muscle to muscle. Both of these can be damaged by twists or wrenching or even by direct blows such as being kicked, tackled or hit by a stick. Where there is either a strain or a sprain it is likely that there is also some damage to the ligaments and/or tendons. This should be treated by a qualified person
- **dislocations** – these only occur at a joint and it is where one bone comes out of its normal position against another. This will also damage the ligaments and tendons. Dislocations often occur at the shoulder, elbow, jaw, thumb and fingers. Telling the difference between this and a fracture is very difficult and it is a job for the experts. You should *never* try to put the dislocated bone back into place.

There are 206 bones in your body, so the chances of breaking one of them is quite high!

Fractures

This is another term for broken bones. They can occur to bones of both the upper and lower body. There are different types:

- **simple or closed** – where the bone is broken but it has not pierced the skin
- **open** or **compound** – where the skin is broken and there is a wound caused by the broken bone which may even be sticking out
- **complicated** – where not only the bone is broken but there is also serious damage to blood vessels or nerves. This can cause heavy bleeding, possibly even more dangerous than the actual break.

Fractures can be caused in various ways and the injured person is likely to be unable to move the damaged limb. Often the sound of the break is heard. Common causes include:

- **impact** – often with another player, through a tackle, a mis-timed kick, being struck with a bat, ball or stick or knocking into a piece of equipment
- **foul play** – this could be through a blow or an illegal tackle
- **accidents** – by falling badly, e.g. while skiing.

Concussion

This is a sudden loss of consciousness and is quite often caused by a blow to the head. You can recognize concussion by the following signs:

- immediate unconsciousness
- very relaxed limbs with a very weak and irregular pulse
- slow and shallow breathing
- large pupils (known as dilated)
- bleeding from the ears – this indicates a very serious injury and must be dealt with as an emergency.

Concussion is considered to be a serious injury and expert medical help must always be sought to deal with it.

The R.I.C.E principle

This term refers to the treatment you should give to injured ligaments or muscles (often known as 'soft tissue injury'). **R.I.C.E.** stands for:

- **R**est – stop straight away and rest the injury. Do not attempt to carry on
- **I**ce – applying ice to the injury reduces swelling and can relieve some pain. Do not apply it directly but use an ice pack
- **C**ompression – this means using either a bandage or some tape which can put some support and pressure to the injured area. Be careful not to apply it too tightly as it could restrict the blood flow
- **E**levation – try to raise the injured part as this will decrease the circulation to the area as it is working against gravity. It also helps to drain away any other fluid from the injury.

You can apply this principle to any injury to the muscles, ligaments or skin as it is a simple but effective treatment.

QUESTIONS

1 What is the difference between a sprain and a strain?
2 What is meant by the R.I.C.E. principle and when should it be used?
3 Describe **three** symptoms of concussion.

5 Fitness for Physical Activities

(a)   The Performer in Action

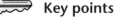 Key points

You need to understand:

- all the body systems included in this section
- how they inter-relate (i.e. work together)
- how they contribute to someone performing in physical activity.

(i)   Skeletal System

 Key points

You will need to know:

- the functions of the skeleton
- specific bones
- specific types of joints
- the names of the different types of body movements
- what cartilage and ligaments do
- how the skeleton is used in performing physical activity.

Functions of the skeleton

There are five distinct functions of the skeleton:

- **Support**   The muscles and many of the softer, delicate vital organs are kept in place by the skeleton. Without it our bodies would collapse.
- **Protection**   It is a protective cover. The skull protects the brain and the ribs protect the heart and lungs. Without it injuries would be far more common and more serious.
- **Movement**   When two or more bones meet there is a joint and this is where movement in the human body occurs. The amount of movement varies between joints.
- **Shape**   As it is the framework of our bodies, the skeleton gives us our human shape. Our muscle and amounts of body fat also contribute to this.
- **Blood cell production**   Red and white blood cells are produced in the bone marrow and mineral salts such as calcium are stored in the bones.

The longest bone in the body is the femur, or thigh bone.

Classification of bones

The human body has four types of bone:

- **long bones** – including the femur, humerus, tibia, fibula, radius and ulna
- **short bones** – including the carpels and tarsals (wrist and ankle bones) and the phalanges
- **flat** or **plate bones** – including the cranium (skull), ribs, pelvis and scapula
- **irregular bones** – including the vertebrae in the spine (vertebral column).

The main bones in the skeleton

This is a diagram of the skeleton showing the most common bones. The ones in bold type are those you need to know about for the exam.

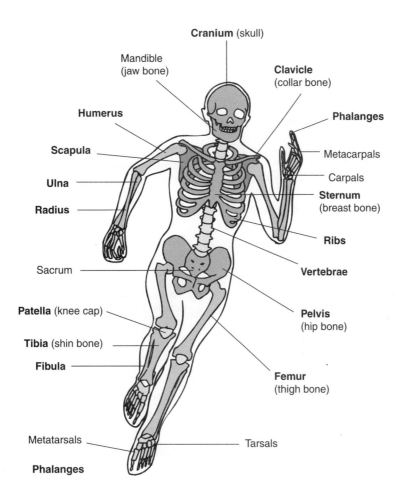

Cranium (skull)

Mandible (jaw bone)

Clavicle (collar bone)

Humerus

Phalanges

Metacarpals

Scapula

Carpals

Ulna

Sternum (breast bone)

Radius

Ribs

Sacrum

Vertebrae

Patella (knee cap)

Pelvis (hip bone)

Tibia (shin bone)

Fibula

Femur (thigh bone)

Metatarsals

Tarsals

Phalanges

Hints and tips

You need to know where the bones in the bold type are located in the body. Make a list of these, study the diagram carefully, close the book and then try to describe where each of the bones on your list is found.

The vertebral column

Key points

You will need to know the functions of the vertebral column (or spine). Also the names, functions and structure of the five regions. These are shown in the diagram below.

There are 33 separate bones in the vertebral column.

Functions of the vertebral column

- to keep the body upright
- to help posture and movement
- to act as a shock absorber
- to protect the spinal cord (this runs down inside the column).

Column regions

1 **Cervical vertebrae** (or **neck**) – seven vertebrae, the top two are known as the atlas and axis. This region allows head movement, such as nodding and shaking, bending and twisting of the neck. The neck muscles are attached here.
2 **Thoracic vertebrae** (or **chest**) – twelve vertebrae which are attached to the ribs and support the rib cage. Some movement takes place to allow bending and turning of the trunk.
3 **Lumbar vertebrae** (or **lower back**) – five vertebrae, the largest of the vertebrae. The back muscles are attached here and the greatest amount of bending, forwards and backwards and side-to-side movement takes place in this region. The most common area for back injuries and should be concentrated on in flexibility exercises.
4 **Sacral vertebrae** – five vertebrae, fused together to form one. Where the spine joins the pelvis.
5 **Coccyx** (or **tail**) – four vertebrae fused together at the very base of the spine.

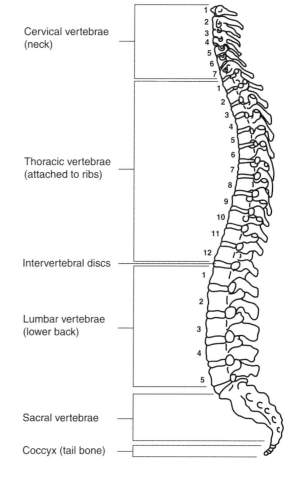

Cervical vertebrae (neck)

Thoracic vertebrae (attached to ribs)

Intervertebral discs

Lumbar vertebrae (lower back)

Sacral vertebrae

Coccyx (tail bone)

The vertebral column (spine)

The coccyx is all that remains of what was the tail before we evolved into humans.

Joints and movement

 Key point

Remember that movement can only occur at a joint. It also requires the combined action of the bones with a pair of muscles for movement to take place.

Types of joint

There are three types:

- immovable (**fibrous** or fixed) – such as the cranium and pelvic bones
- slightly movable (**cartilaginous**) – such as vertebrae of the spine and the pubic bones
- freely movable (**synovial**) – such as gliding, hinge, pivot, condyloid and ball and socket.

Freely movable (synovial) types of joint

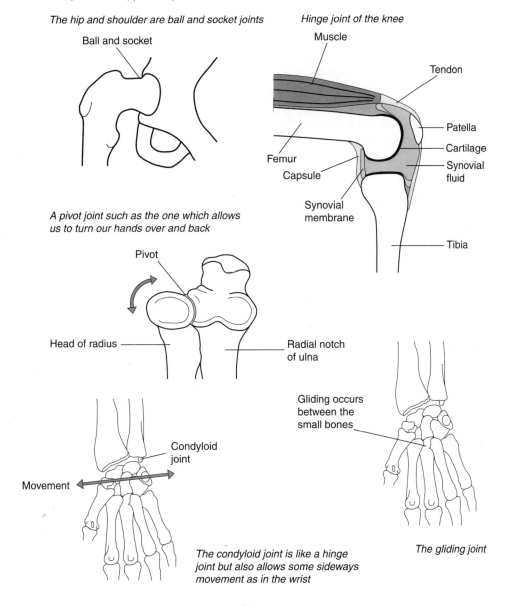

The hip and shoulder are ball and socket joints

Ball and socket

Hinge joint of the knee

Muscle

Tendon

Patella

Cartilage

Synovial fluid

Femur

Capsule

Synovial membrane

Tibia

A pivot joint such as the one which allows us to turn our hands over and back

Pivot

Head of radius

Radial notch of ulna

Gliding occurs between the small bones

Condyloid joint

Movement

The condyloid joint is like a hinge joint but also allows some sideways movement as in the wrist

The gliding joint

Connective tissue

Bones need to be connected in order to allow movement. This is achieved through connective tissue such as:

- **cartilage** – a shiny, smooth, white covering which is very tough and very flexible. It acts as a buffer between the bones at joints, for example, the hyaline cartilage in the synovial joints
- **ligaments** – bands of fibres attached to each of the bones and linking the joints. They help to keep the joints stable and control the amount of movement possible.

Movement definitions

Each movement you make has a particular name. These are the types you need to know and be able to describe:

- **Flexion** – the decreasing of an angle between two bones such as bending the leg at the knee
- **Extension** – when the angle is increased between two bones, such as straightening the leg at the knee
- **Rotation** – where the bone may move round freely in a curve, such as the movement of the arm at the shoulder
- **Abduction** – the movement of a bone or limb away from the body, such as raising the legs upwards and outwards from the hips
- **Adduction** – the movement of a bone or limb towards the body, such as bringing the arms down straight in to the sides of the body from the shoulders.

Hints and tips

The skeleton contributes to movement during physical activity. However, the actual movement occurs as a result of the combined effort of the nervous system, which sends the command to the brain, and the muscular and skeletal systems working together.

QUESTIONS

1 Name **five** functions of the skeleton.
2 Name the **four** different bone classification types and for each one give an example of a bone of that type.
3 Choose **five** different bones in the body and describe exactly where they are located.
4 Name the **five** different regions of the spinal column.
5 Name **three** different types of joints and give an example of each.
6 Name **three** different types of movement and give an example of each.
7 Describe exactly what cartilage and ligaments are.

(ii) Muscles

Key points

You will need to know:

- the three different types of muscles
- specific named muscles and where they are located
- the actions of the muscles (i.e. how they move and allow movement)
- exactly how the muscles are attached to the skeleton.

It is important to remember that any physical movement only occurs through a combined action of the muscles and bones.

There are more than 600 muscles in your body!

Muscle types

There are three types of muscle:

- **voluntary** (or **skeletal**) – sometimes also called striped or striated muscles. They make up the majority of the muscles in the human body. They also give the body its shape. They are called voluntary because they are under your control through the nervous system and only move when you want them to
- **involuntary** (or **smooth**) – muscles you cannot control, such as those in the intestine and the blood vessels. These work automatically all the time to keep your body functioning properly
- **cardiac** – a special type of muscle found only in the wall of the heart. Also a form of involuntary muscle as they work automatically all the time. The beating of the heart is a muscular action which the cardiac muscles perform.

There are around 150 muscles in your head and neck alone!

Muscle groups

There are several areas of the body where muscles are arranged in groups. These are areas where a lot of movement occurs and include:

- **quadriceps** – a group of four muscles at the top front of the leg
- **gluteals** – three main sections of muscle around the buttocks
- **hamstrings** – three muscles at the top back of the legs.

Hints and tips

The majority of the muscles in the body are the skeletal ones and these are shown on the diagrams on page 36. You need to know the names and locations of each of these muscles. Using the list below try to describe exactly where they are on the body. Study the diagrams for some time before you do this and then check your answers.

biceps   triceps   deltoids   pectorals   trapezius   abdominals

latissimus dorsi   gluteals   quadriceps   hamstrings   gastrocnemius

Major skeletal muscles

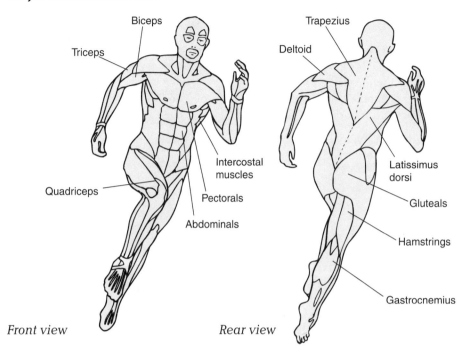

Biceps

Triceps

Trapezius

Deltoid

Intercostal muscles

Quadriceps

Pectorals

Abdominals

Latissimus dorsi

Gluteals

Hamstrings

Gastrocnemius

Front view   *Rear view*

Muscles and movement

Muscles can only pull. They cannot push and they have to work in pairs for any movement to take place. These pairs work by one of the muscles contracting (becoming shorter) while the other one relaxes (becoming longer). This causes movement at the joint around which the two muscles are attached.

Depending on the way they move, these muscles are called:

- **prime mover** (or **agonist**) – the muscle which contracts to cause the movement. For example, if you bend your arm at the elbow, the agonist is the biceps
- **antagonist** – the muscle which relaxes and lengthens to allow movement. In the example of the arm bent at the elbow, the antagonist is the triceps
- **synergists** – any other muscles which are also helping the prime mover to cause a movement. In the elbow-bending example, it would be the brachialis muscle in the forearm.

For any of this movement to take place, the muscles have to be attached to the bones. These are the terms which apply specifically to muscle attachment:

- **origin** – the end of the muscle which is actually fixed to the bone by tendons. It stays still in its position during movement as the fixed, stable end.
- **insertion** – also fixed to the bone by tendons but it is the part of the muscle which actually moves the most. It is therefore at the opposite end of the muscle to the origin
- **tendons** – very strong cords or bands of connective tissue which join muscle to bone. Some are flat and broad and there can be one or more tendons, depending on the size of the muscle.

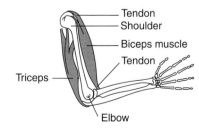

Tendon
Shoulder
Biceps muscle
Tendon
Triceps
Elbow

The muscles of the upper arm, showing how movement occurs at the elbow

Major muscle actions

This list covers all the basic skeletal muscles you need to know, what they do and where to find them. Some of their common names are in brackets:

- **triceps** – at the back of the upper part of the arm, between the elbow and the shoulder. They allow the arm to straighten. Used for throwing actions
- **biceps** – at the front of the upper arm, between the elbow and the shoulder. They allow the arm to bend and also to rotate slightly. Used for catching actions
- **deltoids** – on the back of the shoulder joint. They allow the shoulder to move in all directions, up, down, backwards, forwards and to rotate. These are used greatly in any arm action for swimming
- **pectorals (pecs)** – at the front of the upper chest. They help movement of the shoulders. Used in throwing actions, particularly ones like the javelin
- **trapezius** – by the neck, on the upper back. They help with shoulder movement as well as keeping the shoulder in position. These would be used in a movement such as a soccer throw-in
- **abdominals (stomach)** – at the front on the side of the stomach and across the front. They allow bending and turning of the trunk and also assist with breathing. These are important 'stabilizing' muscles and help the body keep in the correct position for most types of movement
- **latissimus dorsi (lats)** – on the back, from the armpit to the lower back. They allow movement at the shoulder backwards, forwards, up and down, again used in swimming arm actions
- **gluteals** – at the lower back, around the bottom region at the back of the hips. These assist with walking, climbing and standing up as well as rotation of the hips
- **quadriceps (quads)** – at the upper front of the leg in the thigh region, between the knee and the pelvis. They allow the leg to straighten so they assist kicking
- **hamstrings** – at the upper back of the leg, between the knee and the pelvis. They allow movement of the hips and the knee, mainly bending. They also assist kicking
- **gastrocnemius (calf)** – at the back, bottom rear of the leg, between the knee and the foot. They assist with walking, running, jumping and pointing the toes.

QUESTIONS

1. Why are muscles arranged in pairs?
2. Describe the combined actions which take place between muscles and bones to allow physical movements to take place.
3. Name **three** different types of muscle.
4. How are muscles attached to bones?
5. Name **four** different muscles and describe exactly where they are located on the body. For each one describe a physical action it assists in.

(iii) Circulatory System

Key points

You will need to know:

- how to identify and label certain parts of the circulatory system
- details about the heart, blood and blood pressure
- the effects of training upon the circulatory system
- the benefits for performers of having an efficient system.

Functions of the circulatory system

There are three main functions of the circulatory system:

- **transport** – carrying blood, water, oxygen and nutrients throughout the body and the transport and removal of waste
- **body temperature control** – the blood absorbs the body heat and carries it to the lungs and to the skin, where it is then released
- **protection** – it helps to fight disease, e.g. antibodies which fight infection are carried in the blood, also the clotting of blood seals cuts and wounds.

The circulatory system has four main parts:

- the heart
- the blood
- the blood vessels
- the pulmonary and systemic circuits.

Hints and tips

The circulatory system is very closely linked with the respiratory system as it gets the oxygen to the vital organs and removes the carbon dioxide as a waste product.

The heart

The heart is a muscle and, like any other, it contracts and relaxes. Each time it does this it performs a heartbeat. Your pulse is the way you can feel the blood being pumped around by the heart. There are four pulse points in the body:

- at the base of the thumb on the inside of the wrist (**radial pulse**)
- on either side of the neck (**carotid pulse**)
- just over the temple at the side of the forehead (**temporal pulse**)
- in the groin (**femoral pulse**).

Hints and tips

You will need to be able to identify and label diagrams showing those parts of the circulatory system limited to the heart, pulmonary artery and pulmonary vein, aorta, vena cava and capillaries. You will also need to know the direction of the blood flow. The diagrams on the next page give you the information you need.

Your heart beats over a hundred thousand times each day!

The average heartbeat is about 72 times per minute and when you exercise this can increase by up to 3 times!

You have about five litres of blood (about ten pints) in your body and the heart is able to pump it all round your body in less than a minute!

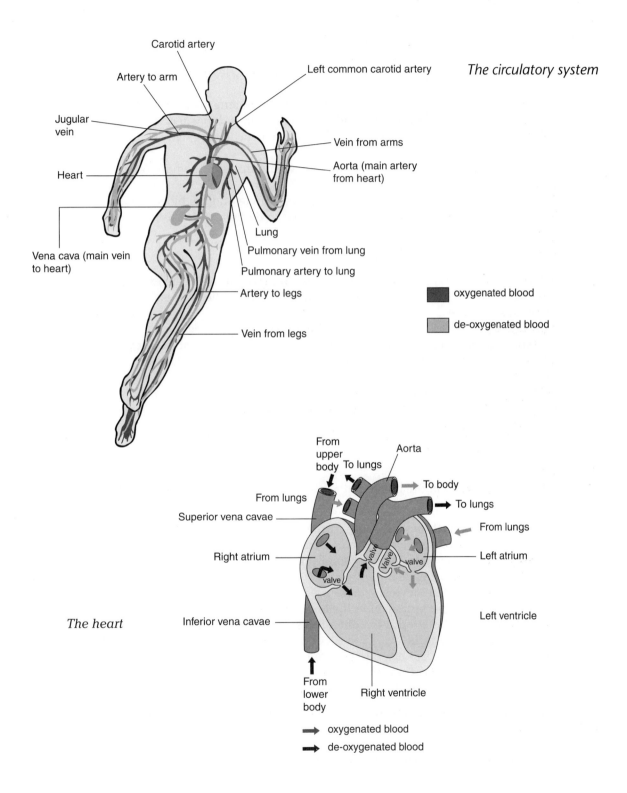

Carotid artery

Left common carotid artery

The circulatory system

Artery to arm

Jugular vein

Vein from arms

Aorta (main artery from heart)

Heart

Lung

Vena cava (main vein to heart)

Pulmonary vein from lung

Pulmonary artery to lung

Artery to legs

Vein from legs

oxygenated blood

de-oxygenated blood

From upper body

Aorta

To lungs

To body

From lungs

To lungs

Superior vena cavae

From lungs

Right atrium

valve

valve

valve

Left atrium

valve

Left ventricle

The heart

Inferior vena cavae

From lower body

Right ventricle

oxygenated blood

de-oxygenated blood

The heart as a pump

The main function of the heart is to act as a pump. This is how it works:

1 The blood enters the right atrium. It is now dark red with little oxygen but mainly waste products such as carbon dioxide.
2 The right atrium pumps the blood into the right ventricle, through a one-way valve.
3 The right ventricle pumps the blood through the pulmonary artery to the lungs where oxygen is picked up and carbon dioxide is deposited. The blood now changes colour to bright red because it is carrying extra oxygen.
4 From the lungs the blood returns to the left atrium through the pulmonary vein.
5 The left atrium pumps the blood into the left ventricle and the blood leaves here through the aorta to be distributed to the rest of the body.

Blood vessels

The blood flows through different blood vessels. These are:

- **arteries** – these carry the blood at high pressure away from the heart and they have the thickest walls. The arteries divide into smaller vessels known as arterioles
- **capillaries** – these are sub-divisions of the arteries and are fed by the arterioles. Capillaries are very thin and known as semi-permeable. They allow carbon dioxide, oxygen, nutrients and waste products to pass through their walls
- **veins** – these are thinner than arteries but with the same structure and they transport the blood back to the heart.

Remember, blood pressure is measured by how much pressure is put on the artery wall by the blood actually flowing through it.

The blood

Cells make up 45 per cent of the blood and are its 'solid section'. There are three types:

- **red blood cells (erythrocytes)** – these are extremely small but there are so many that they give the blood its red colour. They are produced in the bone marrow and contain haemoglobin. It is this that transports the oxygen and carbon dioxide
- **white blood cells (leukocytes)** – these are not so plentiful as red blood cells but they are also produced in the bone marrow and in the lymph tissue. Their main function is to fight against infection and they engulf foreign bodies or bacteria
- **platelets** – these help the blood to clot and are small fragments or particles of larger cells. They not only clot to seal the skin but also do the same job on blood vessels that are damaged.

The remaining 55 per cent of the blood is made up of **plasma** which is the liquid part. It is mainly composed of water but it also contains fibrinogen, protein (which helps in clotting) and nutrients (such as glucose), amino acids, waste products (such as urea) and some carbon dioxide and oxygen.

Up to 2 million red blood cells are produced and destroyed every second!

Effects of training on the circulatory system

Unlike systems such as the muscular one, it is not possible to isolate the specific parts of the circulatory system. However, like any other muscle, the heart will respond to increased levels of exercise by improving its efficiency and pumping the blood around the body more effectively.

Using the principle of overload (see page 54), it is possible to perform vigorous exercise which increases the pulse rate. If you keep working at this level, it will have a benefit on your respiratory system, making it work more efficiently.

You can work at different levels which all have an effect on the circulatory system. These are all related to your pulse rate:

- **maximum pulse** – this is worked out by taking your current age away from 220 and is the absolute highest level that you should achieve
- **training zone** – this is the approximately 80–90 per cent of your maximum rate and is the level to which your pulse should be raised and maintained for maximum benefit
- **aerobic zone** – this is approximately 60–80 per cent of your maximum pulse rate. Whilst beneficial, it is not as intensive or effective as the training zone.

 Key point

Regularly exercising/training in the training zone level will increase the capacity and effectiveness of your circulatory system. The recommended time to achieve benefits is at least fifteen minutes.

The following are the effects which exercise has on the circulatory system:

- **heart/pulse rate** – this increases greatly and can easily double
- **heat production** – there is an increase in body temperature and heat is produced. Due to this, you sweat to help keep the body temperature stable
- **blood pressure** – this increases as more blood is circulated
- **skin colour** – the blood vessels at the surface of the skin have to open up to allow the heat to escape and this can cause a flushed or reddening effect, often seen on the face.

QUESTIONS

1 What are the **three** main functions of the circulatory system?
2 Which is the most important of the **three** functions in your opinion? Why?
3 What is the link between the circulatory system and the respiratory system?
4 What is the **main** function of the heart?
5 Name the **three** different types of blood vessels and briefly describe the function they perform.
6 Name the **three** different types of blood cells and for each one describe what they do.
7 What is plasma and what is it made up of?
8 Describe the way in which you could make the circulatory system more efficient and also describe the effects which exercise has on the system.

(iv) Breathing

Key points

You will need to be able to identify and label diagrams of the breathing and respiratory systems and also to state what the functions of the different parts of the systems are.

Because breathing and respiration are very closely linked – respiration is what happens as we are breathing – the questions at the end of the section refer to both.

The breathing system consists of the following:

- the air passages
- the lungs
- the diaphragm.

These can be seen on the following diagram:

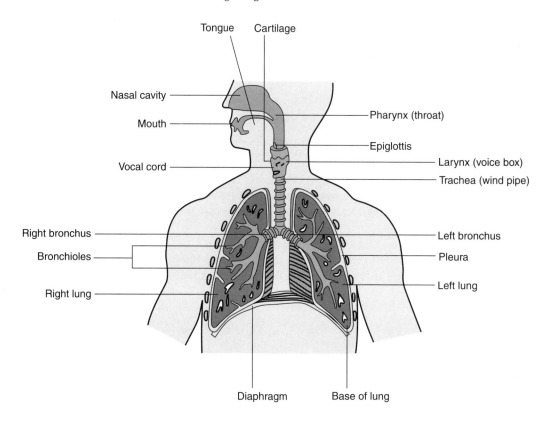

The respiratory system showing the air passages and lungs

The air passages

These are made up of the following:

- **nasal cavity** – air enters into the nasal cavities through the nostrils
- **mouth** – air also enters through here and is separated from the nasal cavity by the palate. This allows you to chew food at the same time as you breathe
- **pharynx** – allows both food and air to enter. The food goes into the oesophagus and the air goes through the **larynx**
- **trachea** – also known as the windpipe. This is a tube consisting of rings of cartilage. Although it is rigid, the cartilage rings are flexible and keep it open
- **bronchus** – at the base of the trachea, where it branches out into two smaller tubes known as the left and right bronchus or bronchi
- **bronchioles** – the bronchi branch out into smaller tubes known as bronchioles and these subdivide into smaller air sacs known as **alveoli**. There are millions of these and they make up the majority of the lung tissue. It is here that the exchange of oxygen and carbon dioxide takes place.

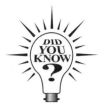

The condition known as bronchitis gets its name from the bronchus where it occurs.

> ### Hints and tips
> Although you need to know about the air passages and their role in getting air into the lungs in the exam, you will only be asked specific questions on the **trachea** and **alveoli**.

The lungs

These are the main organs of the breathing system. They are inside the chest cavity and are protected by the ribs at the back sides and front and by the diaphragm at the bottom. (This is one of the best examples of the skeletal system performing a protective function, see page 30.)

The ribs are like two balloons. There is a slight difference in size between the two as the right lung is a little larger with three sections (or lobes), while the left has only two sections.

The lungs are surrounded by a layer of membrane called the **pleura** which acts as a lubricant. It is smooth and moist and protects the lungs from any friction as they get bigger and smaller during breathing when they expand and contract.

The illness known as pleurisy is named after the area of the lungs, the pleura, where it occurs.

The diaphragm

This is a large muscle sheet which seals off the chest cavity from the abdominal cavity. By contracting and relaxing, it is also responsible for the action of breathing. It combines its movements with those of the intercostal muscles and the ribs which also move in order to allow the action of breathing to occur.

The action of breathing

Breathing involves two types of movement:

- **Inspiration**   As you breath in, your chest cavity changes shape and size. The diaphragm changes from a dome shape, flattens and moves downwards. At the same time the intercostal muscles raise the ribs and push out the sternum (also known as the breastbone), which makes the cavity larger. This reduces the pressure inside the chest cavity and causes air to be sucked into the lungs.
- **Expiration**   As you breathe out, the reverse procedure takes place. The diaphragm relaxes and so do the intercostal muscles. Because of this, the chest cavity returns to its normal size and the pressure on the lungs is increased which forces the air out.

Hints and tips
For the exam, you will need to know how the actions of the diaphragm, intercostal muscles and ribs combine in the action of breathing.

At rest you breathe about 14–16 times per minute but when you exercise it increases with what is called 'forced breathing'. This can raise it by anything up to 50 times a minute!

Types of lung capacity

Your lung capacity will change depending upon whether you are exercising or not. There are two types that you need to know about specifically for the exam:

- **tidal volume** – the amount of air which you breathe in and out normally. This increases with exercise
- **vital capacity** – the largest volume of air which can be expired after the deepest possible inspiration. There is a slight decrease in this during exercise.

It is possible to measure your breathing capacity using a device known as a **spirometer** which can give a read-out of the amount of air you are able to breathe out.

Gaseous exchange

This is the process which allows oxygen to be taken from the air and to be 'exchanged' for carbon dioxide in the body in the following way:

1 Oxygen, which has been breathed in, passes through the alveoli air sacs and into the red blood cells.
2 The oxygen combines with the haemoglobin to form oxyhaemoglobin.
3 An enzyme in the red cells breaks down the carbon dioxide and turns it into a gas.
4 The carbon dioxide gas then passes back through the alveoli and is breathed out through the lungs.

(v) Respiration

> **Definition**
> Respiration is the process in living cells of releasing energy from food molecules.

A top quality international 100-metre sprinter will not breathe at all during a race. They will take one breath at the start and not breathe in again until the finish!

Respiration and breathing are very closely linked. Because of this, the questions at the end of this section refer to both.

Key points

The key terms you must understand from this section are **aerobic** and **anaerobic** respiration.

Anaerobic respiration

This is respiration in the absence of oxygen and is summarized as:

$$glucose \rightarrow lactic\ acid + energy$$

Anaerobic respiration is used only in short bursts and for short periods, for example, by sprinters, or for any activities which require only short bursts of energy. As oxygen is not being used as the main source of energy it is, in fact, being replaced by ATP (adenosine triphosphate).

Aerobic respiration

This is respiration with the use of oxygen and is summarized as glucose + oxygen = carbon dioxide + water + energy. It is used when the body is continuing with activity for a long period of time and the energy to do so is produced with oxygen. Endurance athletes, such as long distance runners or marathon runners, will use this form of respiration.

One of the main reasons for having a warm-down is to help disperse the lactic acid so that it does not build up in the muscles and cause soreness and stiffness in them.

Oxygen debt

If you work very hard during a physical activity, you may find that you are out of breath for quite a time after you have finished. This is because your body has needed more oxygen than you were able to supply. You will have been experiencing aerobic respiration and you will have developed oxygen debt. Your body will have been able to keep working using the lactic acid system (anaerobically respiring), where glucose is broken down in the muscle system. Lactic acid is a mild form of poison and can lead to fatigue and tiredness and even soreness in the muscles after exercise.

Recovery after exercise

You should always allow yourself some time to recover after vigorous exercise and you should not just stop still or collapse to the ground. It is much better to keep moving slowly and gradually, allowing your body to recover and to get your breath back.

Hints and tips
As with the circulatory system, training benefits the breathing/respiratory system by improving its efficiency. The two systems working together are known as the cardiovascular system. Making these systems more efficient improves the level of your cardiovascular endurance.

Effects of training on breathing/respiration

Vigorous exercise (such as in a training session) has the following effects:

- **breathing rate** – this will increase greatly, up to three times the resting rate. The breathing becomes noisier and more obvious and the rate can rise so high that you are literally gasping for breath
- **VO$_2$** (or oxygen uptake) – this increases greatly. The body needs more oxygen so the uptake has to increase to cater for this. In simple terms, the more activity you do, the more oxygen you need but this can only go up to certain maximum levels. When you are at your limit you have achieved your VO$_2$ maximum
- **oxygen debt** – you will develop oxygen debt after about five minutes or more of constant exercise
- **vital capacity** – this will increase as the volume of air required has increased
- **tidal volume** – this increases only slightly.

Fitness testing

There are various methods of testing the efficiency of the breathing and respiratory system which include the following:

- **Multi-stage fitness test** (also known as the 'progressive shuttle run' or 'bleep test') – designed to be a general test of endurance and with the use of various tables, this tests a performer's VO$_2$ maximum. It is easy to set up and administer. All you need is a cassette tape player and an area (preferably indoors) at least 20 metres long. The test consists of a tape recording which has a set of pre-recorded bleeps on it, at various intervals. The people who take part in the test line up at the start point and run to a distance 20 metres away, then run back again. This must be in time with the electronic bleeps on the pre-recorded tape, so they have to run at the pace the bleeps dictate. At the start this is quite easy because the bleeps are quite a long time apart, but every minute they change levels and the time between the bleeps decreases! This means that the performers still have to run the 20 metres but, as each level changes with each minute, they have to speed up. There are 25 levels in all but performers are at sprinting speed long before that. The longer a performer is able to continue – and they must turn after each 20-metre run in time with the tape – the higher their level of endurance. If they turn after the bleep has gone on three consecutive occasions they must stop, so they are not allowed to run at a slower pace.

The multi-stage fitness test was originally designed to test fitness but is now often used as a method of training. Performers carry it out on a regular basis to improve their endurance levels by trying to get a little further each time they take the test!

- **Cooper test** – this is a test of aerobic capacity, or VO$_2$ maximum, so it does the same thing as the multi-stage fitness test. One of the main advantages of this test is that it is easy to set up and do because it does not require any specialist equipment. All you need is a stopwatch and a marked-out running area. It involves running for twelve minutes around the marked-out area and making a note of how far you get in that time. The results can then be used in two ways. You can chart your own progress by keeping a record of how far you get each time and any increases in distance covered will show that you are improving your cardiovascular endurance. Alternatively, you can compare your performance to a chart which links ages and distances covered.

- **Harvard step test** – this is a test of pulse recovery rate which gives a general indication of fitness levels: the quicker your pulse returns to its normal resting rate, the greater your level of cardiovascular endurance. This test is also quite easy to set up and administer. All you need is a bench (or step or block which is about 50 centimetres high), a stopwatch and some paper and a pen to record the results. Before doing the test, you need to make a note of your resting pulse rate. To take the test you do step-ups on the bench continuously for five minutes, at a rate of thirty per minute. You can use a metronome to help with this or find someone to count out every two seconds to keep the pace constant. At the end of the five-minute period you make a note of your pulse rate at intervals as you are recovering: after one, two and three minutes, and you record each of these numbers. You then do a calculation which gives you a score which you can match to a table. The test is based on the fact that the quicker your recovery rate after taking part in strenuous activity, the higher your level of cardiovascular endurance.
- **Cycle ergometer test** – there are various versions of this test that involve cycling on an exercise cycle (known technically as an ergometer) whilst being connected up to a variety of testing equipment. This monitors the amount of air being breathed into and out of the lungs. This test involves the use of very specialized scientific equipment and although it can give extremely accurate results, it is not easily available.

QUESTIONS

These questions refer to Sections (iv) Breathing and (v) Respiration as the two are very closely linked.

1 What does the breathing system consist of?

2 What is the trachea and what is it constructed of?

3 What are the alveoli? What important function do they perform?

4 What do you understand by the terms *tidal volume* and *vital capacity*?

5 Describe what is meant by anaerobic respiration and give an example of a physical activity where it would be used.

6 Describe what is meant by aerobic respiration and give an example of a physical activity where it would be used.

7 What is oxygen debt?

8 What effects can training have on the breathing/respiratory systems?

9 Fully explain and describe a fitness test which is linked to the breathing system.

(vi) Muscular Endurance

Definition
Muscular endurance is the ability of a muscle, or a group of muscles, to keep working against a resistance.

 Key points

You will need to:

- define muscular endurance
- describe when it is required in particular physical activities
- know the ways in which it can be improved, developed and tested.

Hints and tips

The amount of dynamic strength you have relates to the amount of muscular endurance you have. (Dynamic strength is the muscular strength a sportsperson has to support their own body weight over a prolonged period of time, or to be able to apply some force against some type of object.)

When a muscle is no longer able to continue working properly (i.e. it can no longer contract and relax against a load), muscular fatigue takes place and the muscle will literally not be able to work against, or hold, a load any longer. Signs of lack of muscular endurance can soon set in. Muscles begin to ache and feel tired, limbs feel heavy and even the most determined performer has to stop.

You can improve muscular endurance by increasing dynamic strength and the most common way of doing this is through weight training methods.

The need for muscular endurance
Nearly all physical activities require muscular endurance and the chart below gives some examples of where it is needed in particular sports or events.

It is quite easy to check muscular endurance and feel the effects of fatigue. Just hold out a weight, such as a bag of sugar, with your arms out straight in front of you and see how long you can hold it in this position.

Sport/activity	Muscular endurance requirement
Marathon running	Moving the body weight during the 26 miles 385 yards race
Tennis	Being able to hold and swing the tennis racket throughout a match
Pole vault	Carrying and supporting the pole in the run up
Weight lifting	Holding the weight above the head
Rugby	Maintaining the held position in the scrum
Gymnastics	Holding a fixed position such as the rings or pommel horse

Means of improving muscular endurance

There are various exercises which can help to build up muscular endurance in specific muscles or muscle groups. These include the following:

- **sit-ups** – these improve the muscular endurance of the abdominal muscles but it is important that they are performed properly, with the knees bent at right angles and with the hands either clasped across the chest or with the fingertips just touching the ears. You should not clasp your hands behind your head
- **dips** – these need to be done using parallel bars or at the dips station of a weight training room. The body weight is held up supported by the arms and you have to lower yourself by bending the arms at the elbow, until the arm is at right angles, and the arms are then straightened back up again
- **press-ups** – these are easy to do but must be performed correctly. The weight should be taken on the arms and toes with the body laid out in a flat position and the body should be raised and lowered by the bending of the arms. The back should be kept straight and the chest should just brush against the floor before being pushed back up again
- **chins** – this involves using a chin-up bar and can be performed either with an under or over grip. The whole body weight should be suspended and lifted up so that the chin is level with the bar. It should then be lowered so that the arms are hanging completely straight before the body is raised up again.

One important thing to remember is that these exercises need to be performed properly. There is a tendency either to not move the muscle through the full range of movement, or to not keep the body in the correct position, both of which will greatly reduce the effectiveness of the exercise!

There are also specialist weight training facilities and machines which can be used to isolate particular muscles, or muscle groups and these are increasingly popular as a means of improving muscular endurance.

Testing muscular endurance

Muscular endurance is fairly easy to test because it can be worked out by seeing how many times you can do an exercise – known as repetitions.

One of the easiest of these is the sit-up test. You do correct sit-ups, with your knees bent at right angles, and your feet firmly on the floor – sometimes it is easier to have a partner hold your feet down firmly in position. You perform as many sit-ups as you can and record the score. This will give you an indication of the muscular endurance levels of your abdominal muscles. Other tests can easily be worked out for other exercises or equipment.

QUESTIONS

1 Define what is meant by muscular endurance.
2 How can muscular endurance be improved or developed?
3 Describe a sporting situation where muscular endurance is required, explaining how and when it is used or needed.
4 Describe a test for the muscular endurance of a particular muscle group.

(vii) Muscular Strength

> **Definition**
> Strength is the ability of a muscle, or a group of muscles, to overcome a force or resistance.

Key points

You must be able to define strength generally as well as identify the different types of strength. You must also know when muscular strength is needed, identify the sports/events when it is required, as well as ways of improving it and testing for it.

Types of strength

There are very specific types of strength and these include:

- **static strength** – the greatest amount of force which can be applied to an immovable object
- **explosive strength** – muscular strength used in one short, sharp movement
- **dynamic strength** – the muscular strength a sportsperson needs to support their own body weight over a prolonged period of time, or to be able to apply some force against an object. (This type of strength is obviously very similar to muscular endurance.)

The need for muscular strength

A certain amount of strength is needed by all sports performers. They may have to use different types of strength in different phases, or parts, of their performance. The chart below gives some examples of where it is used in particular sports or events.

There is often an argument about what being strong involves. One argument is that it is related to whoever can lift the largest amount of weight. The other is that it should be about how strong someone is in relation to their own body weight.

Sport/activity	Strength requirement
Sprinting	Explosive strength used at the start from the blocks
Tennis	For power in shots such as the serve and volley
Hockey	For generating the power to strike the hockey ball hard
Swimming	To enable you to hold and tow another in a rescue situation
Rugby	For lifting another player up in a line out situation
Gymnastics	In order to hold a handstand position steadily and firmly

Hints and tips

Remember that it is very rare that only one type of strength is being used in an activity. Most actions involve a combination of types of strength.

Means of improving muscular strength

Developing and improving muscular strength is relatively easy as long as you follow the right training programme and understand the principles of training. The most important one here is that of overload (see page 54), as it is vital that the training involves putting an extra stress on the muscle (or muscle group) in order to force it to adapt, with the resultant increase in strength.

In recent years there has been a rise in the number of gyms where strength can be developed. There has also been an improvement in the equipment and facilities available. Previously, the only way to weight train was to use weights on bars known as 'free weights'. These have to be frequently changed, and it is necessary to work with others who can help to load and unload and supervise the lifting.

The new, purpose-built equipment means that people can train on their own with equipment which is safe and easily and quickly adjusted. This new equipment can also be much more specific to certain muscles, or muscle groups, so it is easier to work on the areas you want to.

It is also possible to perform exercises such as those found in circuit training which use the body weight as resistance in order to improve strength. A simple movement such as a squat can use the upper body weight as the resistance in order to increase the strength of the quadriceps muscles.

Hints and tips

You need to be able to distinguish between muscular endurance (the ability of a muscle to keep working against a resistance) and muscular strength (the ability to overcome a force or resistance). The main difference is clearly that of the time element.

Testing muscular strength

Strength can be a difficult thing to test because it is often related to body weight and shape. Body size can be a dominating factor when it comes to testing for static strength. The following tests are for checking explosive strength:

- **standing broad jump** – where you stand with feet together and jump forward as far as possible, measuring the distance covered
- **sergeant jump** – a vertical jump which measures the difference between a person's maximum stretch height and the distance they can then add to it by jumping up vertically.

QUESTIONS

1 Define what is meant by strength.
2 Name **three** specific types of strength and for each one give an example of when it could be used in a sporting situation.
3 What is the difference between muscular strength and muscular endurance?
4 Explain and describe a test you could use for muscular strength. Would this test be fair for all people, regardless of their build or size?

(viii) Flexibility

Definition
Flexibility is the range of movement around a joint. It is also sometimes referred to as suppleness or mobility.

Key points
You should be able to:

- define flexibility
- describe the ways in which flexibility can be achieved and improved
- describe ways in which improved flexibility can help a performance.

The need for flexibility
Having an increased range of movement, and therefore increased flexibility, has the following advantages:

- **Less chance of injury**   Most physical activities require performers to reach or stretch. Quite serious injuries can occur if you stretch too far. A hooker in rugby needs flexibility in the shoulders to bind on to the lock forwards; a tennis player needs it to be able to stretch and reach for shots; and a cricket or rounders player needs it to be able to bend and stretch when fielding.
- **Preparing the body for performance**   Flexibility exercises should be performed immediately before participating as part of the warm-up. This can not only reduce the chances of an immediate pull or strain but also means that the performer is properly prepared for taking part.
- **Improving body posture**   Good posture means that the muscles are holding the body in position correctly and that there are no over-tight muscles which can cause aches and pains.
- **Better, more improved performance**   With a full range of movement at the joints all performances will be improved. In many activities you cannot perform some of the movements without flexibility, for example in gymnastics. In others you become more efficient – a swimmer performing butterfly stroke is a good example of this. Greater flexibility means a sprinter's stride length will increase, and a trampoline performer will be able to perform their routine with greater agility.

Hints and tips
Remember that flexibility occurs only around the joints. It is not to do with how your bones can bend because they cannot! It is the flexibility of the muscles around the joint which allow the movement.

Ways of improving flexibility
Everyone has a certain degree of flexibility but your range of movement can usually be improved. All flexibility exercises need the joints to be moved as far as possible. This can only happen if the muscles surrounding them contract

There is no such thing as being double-jointed. People who can bend their bodies into very tight shapes have extreme ranges of flexibility which allow them to bend their limbs much further than normal.

For activities such as gymnastics and trampolining, you are awarded marks in competitions for the way in which you perform the movements. These are, in effect, marks for the degree of flexibility you have.

and if they are able to work against some kind of resistance which is pushing back against the muscles. These are examples of ways to improve flexibility:

- **static stretching** – you extend a limb beyond its normal range and hold that position for at least ten seconds. You then rest for a short time and repeat the stretch. For maximum effect you would repeat this about five times
- **active stretching** – you extend a limb beyond its normal limits using the momentum of the movement to gain the stretch. This can involve some bobbing type of movements. However, these are becoming increasingly less popular and are being discouraged because if they are not performed carefully, they can lead to overstretching with a sudden strain which can damage muscles
- **passive stretching** – this is where you bend or stretch as far as possible pushing against something. Then you try gradually to push further and further to increase the range. Sometimes a coach can help you to push, but this must be done very carefully.

Any stretching movement will help you to increase your flexibility and you must try to hold the stretch for about ten seconds each time you do so. You should also remember to work on the most important areas, such as the shoulders and arms, back, hips and legs. Wherever you have a joint you can perform flexibility exercises!

Testing flexibility

Testing flexibility is fairly simple and doesn't require a lot of expensive equipment. It is quite easy to perform flexibility exercises and keep a record of the amount of movement achieved.

The most common test is known as the 'sit and reach' test. You sit down with your feet straight out against a block or bench. You place your fingers on the top of the block (or a slide bar if you have one) and measure the distance that you can slide your fingers forward. This tests the amount of flexibility in the lower back and hamstrings.

Hints and tips
There is a link between strength and flexibility. Often, if you increase strength greatly you also increase the bulk and size of the muscles and this can reduce flexibility. That is why it is always important to include flexibility exercises as part of your training programme to reduce this possible effect.

QUESTIONS

1 Define what is meant by flexibility.
2 Why should you include flexibility exercises in your warm-up?
3 How can increased flexibility help to improve a performance? Give some examples.
4 How can you improve flexibility?
5 Explain and describe a test for flexibility.

(b) Fitness Training
(i) Understanding of Terminology and Principles

Key points

It is important to know all of the terms associated with training and to understand how they can be used to set an effective training programme. This is a theory area which you may have to put into practice when planning, performing and evaluating your own training programme.

The principles of training

The reason for training is to improve your ability to take part in physical activity. This improvement can only come about through a change and you may be trying to make a physical change. It is, therefore, very important that you are aware of the body systems which will be affected and other factors which can affect your ability to train successfully.

Training has certain principles which apply no matter what type you undertake. It is important to know what they are, the correct terminology and the effects they will have. The main principles of training are:

- **Specificity**   Any training must be suitable, or specific, to the physical activity or sport you are training for. It would not be wise to choose a strength-training programme if you were hoping to build up to running a marathon. You may wish not only to choose one particular type of training but also to concentrate on one particular area. It may mean building up strength in the legs or the arms, or increasing flexibility in the shoulders, or making reaction times improve. Specific exercise will produce specific results and this must be considered with two other points:
  - individuals will respond differently to the same methods
  - each activity will have different, and specific demands.
- **Overload**   This is making the body work harder in order to improve it. You will have a 'capacity' to train which will be the normal level you work at. In order to improve you must extend that capacity by increasing your workload and your body will respond by adapting to it. This can be achieved in the following ways:
  - **frequency** of training needs to be increased. To start with you may only train twice a week with a recovery period in between, but this could be increased to every other day and then up to five days a week. Top performers would probably train on some aspect of their activity every day. However, it does not necessarily help to have more than one session in a day – just one is more advisable
  - **intensity** must be increased. You can do this by simply working harder at the training method you are using. You might want to increase your heart rate to a higher level or just to add more weight if you are trying to increase strength
  - **duration** may refer to the length of each training session, which should be increased. It can also be the amount of time you spend on a particular aspect of your training.

- **Progression**   The training you are doing, and particularly the amount of overload, must be increased progressively. In other words, as your body adjusts to the increased demands which you are putting upon it, so that demand must be steadily increased. If you stay at the same levels, the improvement will not continue but you must be careful not to do too much too soon. If you do, it may lead to injury or muscle damage which will then set your training programme back. There is also a factor known as **plateauing** which means that you get to a certain level and then stop making progress. You can be stuck for some time at this level before you are eventually able to progress again.
- **Reversibility**   Just as progression can lead to an improvement, if you either stop or decrease the amount of training, you go into reverse and lose the effect – all the good work you have done will be lost! Sometimes you cannot avoid stopping if you have an injury or if you are ill, and you must accept that your training programme will have suffered a setback.

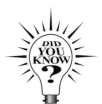

A three-week break in training can result in a ten per cent loss of the effects you have gained. Some performers have claimed that having one month off from training takes two months to recover to the previous levels.

Terminology of training

There is also specific terminology relating to training. You must know:

- **repetitions** – the number of times you repeat a particular movement within an exercise. If you were weight training, it would be the number of times you moved the weights. If you were circuit training it might be, for example, the actual number of sit-ups or press-ups
- **sets** – this is the number of times you actually do a particular activity (rather than just the movements which make up that activity). If it were weight training it might be the number of times you do a bench press. For circuit training it would be the number of laps you do.

These terms are very closely linked to overload because adjusting the number of repetitions and sets in your training programme will have a great bearing on how effective that training programme will be.

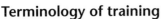

*These principles and terms apply to **all** forms of training not just one. If you were trying to improve your cardiovascular endurance levels you would still use the principle of overload but you would have to increase your heart and breathing rate progressively. If you were trying to increase muscular endurance you would overload particular muscles or muscle groups – also progressively!*

QUESTIONS

1 What do the terms, specificity, overload, progression and reversibility mean?
2 Describe **three** ways you can achieve overload.
3 What is the difference between repetitions and sets?
4 Name an activity and describe the most appropriate type of training for it. In your answer consider how the principles of training could be used to the best advantage.

(ii) Specific Training Methods, Effects on the Body, Safety Factors

 Key points

Only the training methods in this section will be examined. You should know:

- what each of the training methods consists of
- how the training can have the desired effect on the body
- what safety factors specific to each of the training methods should be taken into consideration.

You will also need to be fully aware of the terminology relating to the principles of training which were covered on pages 54–5.

Weight training

Weight training is designed to increase strength and many activities require some form of strength and weight training. Its purpose is to:

- **increase muscle strength** – this involves a programme to increase the size of the muscles and therefore increase their strength. This uses the principle of overload (see page 54) which will stress the muscles, gradually making them bigger. This can be achieved by having heavy weights with small numbers of repetitions, and performing several sets
- **improve muscle tone** – this involves a programme to 'tone up' the muscles without necessarily trying to increase their bulk and size. This can be achieved by using lighter weights, increasing the repetitions (probably somewhere between ten and fifteen times), to a probable maximum of three sets.

There are also more specific ways in which weight, or strength training can be used. Free-standing weights are those which can be fixed on long or short bars. These traditional weights are often preferred by people who want to increase strength because it is easier to add more weight. One of the drawbacks to the weight training machinery is that it does not always have enough weight on it and it is not possible to add more.

If free-standing weights are used it is vital that you do not train alone. You should always have an instructor or training partner with you to help load and unload the weights and to help you start and stop the actual weightlifting movements. For some movements such as the bench press it may even be necessary to have two other people present to lift up the weights for you as you start and lower them down when you have finished.

Circuit training

One of the advantages of circuit training is that it is very adaptable. There are a number of ways in which either an individual or group can use the circuit. The time taken, the amount of work done and the load for each area can all be varied and changed.

The various parts of the circuit are known as stations. It is very important that the stations work properly, following these rules:

- **stations must be clearly marked** with the movement or activity to be performed

- **activities must be demonstrated and/or practised** to make sure they are being performed correctly. For example, you will not get the maximum benefit from a press-up if you do not do it properly. Also, when the circuit is underway a check must be made to ensure that all the activities are being performed correctly
- **activities must be varied around the circuit**. This means that there should not be a group of abdominal muscle exercises arranged together, or any other group of exercises which are similar. They must be spread out at even intervals throughout the circuit, otherwise a performer might fatigue a muscle area by overworking it. Spreading the exercises evenly allows the muscles a little time to recover before they are exercised again, so overload can be more effective. It also makes the circuit less boring if there is a variety of exercises rather than repeating the same ones
- **a recovery period** should be allowed **between each exercise** so that the performers can recover sufficiently to do the next one. Some circuits can last up to 30 minutes and it is unrealistic to expect someone to work constantly at that level for that long.

Types of circuit
There are two main types of circuits:

- **fitness circuits** – these consist of various types of exercises such as press-ups, sit-ups, etc.
- **skills circuits** – as well as exercise stations, there are other stations where specific skills relating to a particular sport are included, such as chest passing against a wall with a basketball, or dribbling in and out of cones with a hockey stick and ball.

Running the circuit
There are various ways to run the circuit:

- **timed circuits** – where performers work for a certain length of time at each station and then rest before going on to the next one (e.g. 30 seconds work, 30 seconds rest)
- **fixed load** – each station is labelled with the amount of work the performer must do (e.g. 15 press-ups each time).

Both these methods can be varied. The number of laps (therefore sets) can be adjusted, or the periods of work or recovery, or the load and skills could be changed.

Interval training
This consists of periods of work followed by periods of rest and is aimed at improving endurance levels. The principle is much the same as for circuit training (which allows a rest period between stations) and prevents the performer from being too fatigued to carry on.

This can be achieved by adjusting the following:

- **duration of the work** – this could relate to how far a performer may need to run or for how long they may work
- **intensity of the work** – the speed at which they work, or the load they have
- **repetitions** – the number of work ones or the number of rest ones
- **duration of the recovery period** – this usually refers to time but it may involve a recovery distance, such as a certain distance a performer is allowed to slow walk.

The two most important factors in interval training are the amount of work related to the amount of rest. There are two types of interval training:

- **long interval training** – this is particularly good for players in team games and middle distance runners as it works in bursts from 15 seconds up to 3 minutes. Work periods are therefore quite long and the performers work at between 80–85 per cent maximum
- **short interval training** – this is designed for short bursts of activity so it would suit sprint athletes or players of, say, racket sports where there is much stop and go action. The work periods are much shorter, no more than 15 seconds but performers work flat out for this period.

Some boxers train in three minute bursts because that is the length of one round of boxing

Continuous training

This is a method of training to improve endurance. Performers take part in an activity which keeps the pulse and heart rate at a high level, for example:

- **running and jogging**
- **cycling**
- **swimming**
- **exercise sessions** (such as aerobic classes).

There are also specialist machines which can be used, such as running treadmills, exercise cycles and rowing machines.

Fartlek training

This is based on a Swedish method of training, it means 'speed training' and is a form of continuous training. It alternates walking, brisk walking, running, jogging and fast steady running. These can all be performed in a session as required so the individual decides when they are ready to build up to a fast run after progressing from a walk.

Multi-stage fitness test

This test is dealt with in detail on page 46. Although it was designed primarily to test levels of endurance and VO_2 maximum uptake, it is being used more and more as a method of training. It can be valuable for increasing cardiovascular endurance levels.

QUESTIONS

1 Describe what weight training consists of. In your answer give details of the different ways that weight training can be used and the benefits of it. Explain specific safety rules which apply to weight training.

2 Describe what circuit training is and explain how it is organized and set up. Draw out a diagram of a typical circuit and describe how it would be run.

3 Explain what interval training is and describe **two** different ways it can be used.

4 Describe what is meant by Fartlek training and explain how it is organized.

5 What are the benefits of using the multi-stage fitness test as a training method?

6 Factors Affecting Performance

(a) Physiological

Key points

You should remember that these are factors which will affect a performance and they are all connected with how your body works (and are therefore physiological).

Lack of sleep

Tiredness can have a very bad effect on performance. It reduces levels of concentration and co-ordination which then reduce the skill levels of the performer. Movements become sluggish and thoughts can often be confused, speech can even be slurred.

This can be a very real problem at the top level in sport if someone is worried or nervous before a big event. This can lead to sleeplessness, not just the night before but over a period of time. This tiredness could then badly affect the eventual performance.

All performers need sufficient rest to be able to perform at their best and getting a reasonable amount of sleep is important.

Fatigue

This is one of the most serious and damaging factors which can affect a performance. It occurs when the body, or parts of the body, get so tired, through the amount of work they have been called on to do, that they stop working properly.

Fatigue can occur in the muscles (see page 48) so that they will not be able to carry on whatever work they are doing. As fatigue sets in it will lead to a decrease in skill levels and the performer will not be able, say, to move the extra yard to intercept a pass or play a shot. More mistakes will be made as the tiredness sets in and the effects get worse, not better.

If the performer tries to keep going without a rest, the chances are they will have to stop completely. There are cases where this has happened even at the top levels in sport. This can be a dangerous condition. Injuries are more likely to occur because of the performer's inability to carry out movements properly. Techniques can also start to suffer.

If fatigue has really set in, the only solution is for the performer to stop before they do themselves harm. It is important that coaches and managers of teams can recognize the signs of fatigue and substitute a player if possible.

Depriving people of sleep has been used as a form of torture. It can bring on a very confused mental state and if carried on can result in quite serious illness.

Fatigue has led to performers completely collapsing from exhaustion because they can no longer carry on.

Effects of smoking

In the UK every packet of cigarettes carries a health warning which must be printed by law. There is no dispute about the fact that smoking is harmful, which is why these warnings have to be printed. The dangers caused by smoking include:

- greater risk of serious illnesses such as heart disease, lung cancer and chronic bronchitis, which are all life threatening
- developing a 'smoker's cough'
- frequent sore throats
- shortness of breath
- nose, throat and chest irritation and breathing difficulties
- headaches
- dizziness, nausea and lack of concentration.

The most dangerous thing about smoking is that it kills. Over 100,000 people a year die as a result of smoking. It kills more people from heart attacks than any other disease. No one who smokes can expect to be healthy or maintain a good level of fitness.

It is generally recognized that if tobacco had only recently been discovered it would almost certainly be outlawed as illegal due to its harmful effects.

Effects of alcohol

Like many other things, moderate amounts of alcohol do not necessarily do any harm. However, if someone drinks too much then the immediate effect is that they become drunk. This can often lead to violent behaviour. It also causes lack of co-ordination and usually vomiting, too. If excessive drinking continues over a period of time there can be more serious effects such as:

- damage to the liver, muscles and heart
- damage to the digestive system
- mental illness such as hallucinations, memory loss, depression, brain damage and extreme confusion
- damage to the immune system, leaving the body less able to fight diseases.

Alcohol is a mood-altering drug. Technically it is a depressant drug as it slows down the action of the brain. Any performer in a physical activity will be affected by alcohol. It is for this reason that you should not drink any alcohol before taking part in physical activity.

Effects of adrenaline

Adrenaline is a hormone which is released from the adrenal gland into the bloodstream causing an increase in heart rate. It also causes an increase in the strength of the heart muscle contraction. This can therefore aid a performance as it can stimulate the respiratory and cardiovascular systems.

Adrenaline is known as the 'fright, fight or flight' hormone because of the effect it has on the body system.

Effects of high altitude training

Some athletes, particularly middle- and long-distance runners, train at high altitudes. This is because at high altitudes, the blood oxygen level decreases which stimulates the body to produce more **erythrocytes** (red blood cells which transport the oxygen and carbon dioxide – see page 40). This will make them more effective performers.

Effects of drugs

Many drugs are illegal and sports organizing bodies have outlawed certain other drugs which they consider to be 'performance enhancing'. That is, they affect performance levels by making them better. These come under the following categories:

- **Stimulants**   These substances increase alertness, reduce fatigue and may increase competitiveness and hostility. They can also cause a loss of judgement and this can lead to accidents in some sports. There is also an unusual group of stimulants known as **beta$_2$agonists** which are classified as being both stimulants and anabolic agents. The side effects can include:
  - high blood pressure and headaches
  - strokes and increased and irregular heartbeats
  - anxiety and tremors
  - insensitivity to serious injuries
  - addiction.
- **Narcotic analgesics**   These include morphine, heroin and codeine. The main reason that they are banned is because they hide the effects of illness and injury. They suppress the feeling of pain and performers must be very careful to draw the line between treating an injury and actually concealing its full extent by taking these drugs. Their side effects are:
  - respiratory depression
  - physical and psychological dependence
  - exhaustion or over-training
  - constipation
  - extreme apathy.
- **Anabolic agents**   These are probably the best known and most commonly abused drugs in sport. The main type is known as **androgenic anabolic steroids**. This is a group of both natural and synthetic compounds which are very similar to the natural male hormone testosterone. Testosterone has the effect of promoting the development of male characteristics and stimulating the build-up of muscle tissue. Performers take them for the following supposed benefits:
  - increasing muscle strength
  - enabling them to train harder and for longer
  - increasing their competitiveness.

Two cyclists are known to have died as a result of taking stimulants and continuing to ride with the effects of fatigue masked by the drugs.

The main benefit seems to be that they can help with training and because of this they are often called 'training drugs'. The risks involved with taking steroids are quite serious and include:

- liver disorders and heart disease, including jaundice, liver failure, liver tumours and bleeding of the liver; the heart can be affected by changes in its fatty substances. This can lead to an increased liability to heart attacks, strokes and increased blood pressure
- sexual and physique problems: in children, growth can be affected or even stunted. Men can suffer from reduced sperm production and sterility. There can be shrinking of the testicles, impotence and even the growth of breasts. Women can have a disruption of the menstrual cycle and ovulation, changes in the sex organs, balding, acne, growth of facial hair and deepening of the voice. Steroids can also cause miscarriage, still birth or damage to the foetus, especially in early pregnancy
- behavioural effects: there can be quite marked changes of behaviour in some individuals. This can be seen as increased moodiness and aggression and can be so extreme they may constitute a psychiatric disorder.

A sprinter who used steroids as a training aid would only need a ten per cent improvement to change from being a borderline international athlete to a world record holder. This seems to be why so many athletes are tempted!

- **Diuretics**   These are used medically to reduce excess body fluids and for the management of high blood pressure. Sports performers could misuse them:
  - to reduce weight quickly in sports where weight categories are important
  - to reduce the concentration of substances by diluting the urine; it is also known as a 'masking agent', hiding other illegal substances in the body.

  Because of this second effect, some authorities reserve the right to obtain urine samples from competitors at the weigh-in prior to a competition.

- **Peptide hormones, mimetics and analogues**   Peptide hormones 'carry messages' around the body to increase growth, influence sexual and general behaviour and to control pain. Analogues are synthetic drugs which have a similar effect. These drugs raise various hormones to abnormal concentrations and the side effects can include:
  - muscle wastage through prolonged use
  - enlarged internal organs
  - unusual growth patterns such as enlarged hands and feet.

- **Beta-blockers**   These are prescribed to people who have a medical condition affecting their heart. They calm and control the heart rate and they are therefore identified as being a benefit in some activities where staying calm can be an advantage. Due to this beta-blockers are totally banned in activities such as archery, shooting and modern pentathlon – all of these activities require a steady hand to aim which obviously could be helped by the effects of the drug.

There was a case where a snooker player had been prescribed beta-blockers for a heart condition and he was banned from his sport because it was thought that taking them gave him an unfair advantage.

- **Blood doping** Some years ago, endurance athletes used this to make their blood more efficient in carrying and supplying oxygen. It involves having a transfusion of blood (this is when blood is actually added back into the bloodstream). It can involve an athlete having blood taken away, training with depleted blood levels, then having the blood replaced. It can even be replaced with someone else's blood, red blood cells or related products. This used to be tolerated, but is now banned. Possible side effects include:
  - development of allergic reactions such as a rash or fever
  - acute kidney damage if the incorrect blood type is used
  - delayed transfusion reaction which can result in a fever and jaundice
  - transmission of infectious diseases such as viruses, hepatitis and AIDS
  - overload of the circulation and metabolic shock.

As well as banning blood doping, there is also a ban on any interference by what is known as pharmacological, chemical and physical manipulation. This covers things such as interfering with urine samples or using medical knowledge to help performers.

High altitude training can have the same benefits as can be gained by blood doping but it obviously does not carry the same risk of dangerous side effects.

QUESTIONS

1 What effects can a lack of sleep have on the body? How could that affect a sporting performance?

2 What is fatigue? What are the problems which may occur if someone is suffering from fatigue and what should be done to deal with it?

3 What harmful effects can smoking have on a performer?

4 What are the short-term and long-term effects of drinking too much alcohol?

5 What is adrenaline and how does it aid a physical performance?

6 What advantages can be gained through high altitude training?

7 Name **three** categories of performance-enhancing drugs. For each one describe the benefits performers think they gain as well as the possible side effects each one might have.

8 What are beta-blockers? Why are they banned in certain sports?

9 Describe what blood doping is and state why athletes might want to use it.

(b) Body types

 Key points

You need to know details about how individuals may vary in terms of their body type, gender and age, and understand that all these factors will affect performance.

Somatotype

This is another word for a body type – and that is the type of body you were born with which is determined genetically. Your body shape can be improved but you cannot make drastic changes to it, such as increasing your height or your basic bone structure. The following body types, or somatotypes, have been identified:

- **endomorph** – people with this basic shape are short and rounded with a tendency to gain weight. They have short legs in relation to their trunks
- **mesomorph** – this body is a basic Y-shape, well muscled with wide flexible shoulders, long arms and hands, a narrow waist and lightweight legs
- **ectomorph** – these people are relatively short with thin arms and shoulders. They often have a small head with a long neck, a short waist and long legs.

Not many people fall clearly into one of these categories. Most people are a mixture of all three.

Somatotype and sport

Your body type can be a very important factor in physical activities because it may mean that you are particularly well suited to one particular sport or unsuited to another.

It makes a lot of sense to identify the activities you are suited to, with your natural advantages, rather than trying to overcome the limitations that your body type might impose. If you are tall then it is an advantage in basketball, high jump and swimming. Shorter people make better gymnasts and it is vital to be short if you want to become a jockey.

There are a lot of activities where you can take part whatever your body type. In rugby, for example, a short, stocky person would be well suited to the front row in the scrum, a tall person would be good as a line out jumper, and a short, light person would be good as a scrum half.

Gender

Whether you are male or female is probably one of the most influential factors in sport. There are real differences between men and women, and this is not an unfair comment – it is true.

The following are affected by gender:

- **strength** – on average women have only two-thirds the strength of men, as men have greater muscle mass. Because men have higher testosterone levels, they have greater muscle growth

There are no Olympic-standard high jumpers who are less than six feet tall and many of them are much taller still. This is because they have a higher centre of gravity in their bodies which gives them an advantage when jumping over the bar.

- **rate of maturity** – girls mature earlier than boys so competition between them when young can be fair. From the age of about eleven, though, boys start to overtake girls in terms of height, weight and strength. Because of this, many sports become single sex from eleven upwards
- **body type** – women have a flatter, broader pelvis (designed for childbearing) and have a higher percentage of body fat. Women also have smaller lungs and heart so this affects cardiovascular endurance levels. Menstruation (periods) can also affect performance.

Age as a factor

This is very important for the following reasons:

- **physical maturity** – very young people are not able to cope with too much information, especially if it is too complicated. They may simply not understand how to do things so tasks to be practised and learnt must be kept simple
- **strength** – maximum strength will not be achieved until late teens or early twenties. It peaks at around 30 and then declines by up to 40 per cent from age 30 onwards
- **diet** – the body metabolism slows down as you get older so there is a tendency to gain weight, especially from the age of 40 onwards
- **oxygen capacity** – this reduces with age. A 50-year-old has a reduced capacity compared with a 20-year-old
- **injury and disease** – the older you get the more likely you are to suffer injuries (and the longer it takes to recover from them). There is also an increased chance of disease, such as heart disease
- **reaction time** – this decreases with age. The very young have very good reaction times
- **skill** – this can improve due to growth (high jumpers and basketball players may appear more skilful as they get taller). Also experience may be an asset and it is only gained over time.

There is only one major sport where women compete against men directly and that is horse riding/jumping. Otherwise all sport is organized specifically, and separately, for men and women.

QUESTIONS

1. Name **three** different somatotypes and for each one suggest a sport which might suit their particular body type.

2. Describe **three** differences between men and women and explain how these might affect their ability to participate in some physical activities.

3. Explain why most sports are arranged in age divisions, especially for juniors. What factors influence this decision?

(c) Acquisition of Skill

Definition
Skill has been defined as, 'when a predetermined objective is accomplished with a minimum outlay of energy'. Put in simple terms, it is a combination of knowledge or expertise. In PE it is the ability to perform activities or movements, with control and consistency, to bring about a desired result, e.g. full control of a ball, a bat or body movements. A skill can be basic or complex, often depending on the type of activity undertaken.

 Key points
This is one of the key areas of your course and it should always be considered in conjunction with the practical work you do. How you learn skills, practise them and the guidance you receive while you are doing so are the key points you must understand.

Types of skills
Skills can be placed in one of two categories:

- **basic skills** – simple things such as throwing, catching, striking, jumping and running
- **complex skills** – these take a longer time to learn and could include catching a fast-moving, hard struck ball, hitting a golf ball with a club, performing the pole vault jump, running in a hurdles race.

Note that the complex skills are all more advanced forms of the basic ones!

Types of practice
Skills can only be learnt through practice which you can do in various ways:

- **skills practice** – here you are working on acquiring particular skills which may be specific to a certain activity. They can be group skills (such as a short corner practice for hockey), or individual skills (such as a tennis player practising their serve). If it is a team activity, it is a good idea to practise both individual and group skills, so for netball you might practise the group skill of the centre pass followed by the individual skill of shooting
- **game situation** – here you practise the skills tried out earlier in a game situation or even a match. This is sometimes a conditioned game where some new or adapted rules are introduced which make it easier to play – or easier to practise some particular skills. Examples of this include allowing players on to the court to serve underarm at tennis to enable the game to get underway better, or to allow goals to be scored at soccer only with headers.

Top performers in any sport will practise their skills every day!

Practice is something which does have to be performed regularly and it should be linked in with training and training sessions.

Open and closed skills

In some sports, certain skills fall into one of these categories:

- **open skills** – these show up in situations which are constantly changing, for example, footballers who are taking part in a match in a constantly changing environment. They may have to change, or adapt, their skills according to the demands of the game. A strong wind blowing could affect them, and team mates and opponents constantly moving around would also be factors
- **closed skills** – these skills have set patterns. For example, a trampolinist performs in an environment that does not change as the equipment used is always the same. There are set moves, shapes and routines. The skills used here, such as somersaults and twists, do not change.

Feedback

The information given to a performer about how a skill has been performed is called feedback. There are various types:

- **continuous feedback** – given throughout a performance, by coach/teacher
- **terminal feedback** – given at the end of a performance
- **knowledge of results** – a form of terminal feedback; may be as simple as whether you won or lost
- **knowledge of performance** – how well you did the performance rather than just the end result
- **internal/intrinsic feedback** – sensed, or felt, by you whilst performing
- **external/extrinsic feedback** – from other sources such as sounds or things you can see
- **positive feedback** – information about successes of the performance
- **negative feedback** – information about unsuccessful performance aspects

Feedback is used to help a performer set further goals for the level of performance they wish to achieve in the future.

Types of guidance

Most guidance is provided by people such as teachers or coaches. This is one of the main ways that a performer receives knowledge of results.

It is difficult for a performer to actually observe themselves while they are performing to check for any faults or areas for improvement. This is why they get other people to analyse their performance. This could even be achieved through using a video recording of the performance.

QUESTIONS

1 Describe what is meant by a simple and a complex skill and give an example of each.
2 What different types of practice are there? How can these practice situations be used to improve the acquisition of skill?
3 What is the difference between an open and a closed skill?
4 What types of feedback are there and why are they important in the learning of skills?
5 Describe the types of guidance a performer might receive. Explain who is likely to give guidance to performers.

(d) Psychological factors

Key points

These are factors which affect your state of mind which can then affect the way you are able to perform. Usually these factors make a performance worse.

Tension

A performer can experience tension personally, in anticipation of an event. It is also an atmosphere which can be generated by spectators. Tension is related to excitement or suspense and it is easy to see how these feelings can be transferred from performers to spectators and back again. Tension can also exist just between two players or teams.

Tension does not always have a bad effect on performance. Some competitors find that they cannot compete properly unless there is some tension, and they respond to it positively. Others find that tension makes them nervous and uncertain and this results in a poor performance.

Anxiety

A person who is anxious is uneasy or troubled and clearly this is not a good state for a performer to be in. All performers experience some level of anxiety before or during a performance and, to some extent, this is not only normal but it can actually help.

However, when a player becomes over-anxious, or nervous, their performance can get worse, especially if they are already in a tense situation.

The main reason why someone feels anxious is that they are worried about losing or performing badly. This is made even worse if people they know are watching them.

Boredom

When you are bored you are totally uninterested in what you are doing, your concentration lapses and the chances are that you will try very little – if at all!

It is unusual to be in a sporting situation which is boring by choice but boredom can set in if you are being unsuccessful. It will lead to a decrease in the standard of your performance.

Motivation

This is the amount of determination a performer has to do well. Highly motivated players are more likely to cope with anxiety, tension, boredom, stress and pressure because they are positive about what they are doing and they want to succeed. Some people can be motivated just by the desire to win. For others it is the rewards that go with winning, such as money and fame, which are more important.

It is probably more difficult to motivate people who are used to winning because of this. They have become used to being the best so it can be difficult for them to motivate themselves sufficiently to stay at the top. This is why top sportspeople often employ a personal coach or trainer to help, not only with their physical preparation, but also with their mental preparation and motivation as well.

Personality and sport

The type of person you are can have an influence on the type of sport you are likely to take up and the way in which you take part in it. There are two particularly identified personality types:

- **introverts** – people who are quiet and self-centred, not high in confidence, not looking to lead
- **extroverts** – people who are confident and outgoing with a high opinion of themselves, often leaders.

Extroverts perform better at a higher level of arousal; *introverts* perform better at a lower level.

Extroverts tend to favour team games; *introverts* prefer individual activities or ones requiring fine physical skills.

Extroverts favour activities with varied outcomes and plenty of action such as any invasion game; *introverts* favour ones with little variety and more certain outcomes such as cross-country running or distance swimming.

Extroverts have been shown to have greater pain tolerance so are suited to any contact sport, or one which allows contact.

Due to their leadership qualities, *extroverts* are more likely to adopt roles such as captaining teams.

Aggression in sport

Aggression is recognized as a personality trait (an aspect of your personality) and many sports, especially contact ones such as soccer and rugby, encourage what is known as 'controlled aggression'. If it is controlled it can be quite an advantage for performers. However, if they are unable to control it, they are likely to be in trouble with officials.

One of the penalties the football authorities have used is to play matches behind closed doors with no spectators admitted. This is so that some of the psychological advantages associated with tension and motivation are removed!

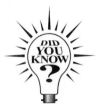

The majority of professional sportspeople are likely to be extrovert personality types due to the fact that they have to perform in front of large crowds and audiences.

QUESTIONS

1 Explain how the following factors may affect a sporting performance: tension, anxiety and boredom.

2 Describe what is meant by motivation. How can it help a performer to do well in a sporting situation?

3 Explain what is meant by extrovert and introvert personality types. What types of activities would each be most suited to?

4 What is meant by 'controlled aggression' and in which activities might it be used to advantage?

Section B: Sport and Society

7 Local and National Issues

(a) Sponsorship

 **Key points**

The issue of sponsorship is a large and constantly changing one. Questions regarding it often refer to advantages and disadvantages to individuals and the sports in general. It is very useful to keep yourself up to date with issues regarding sponsorship which are often covered in the media.

What is sponsored?
Today sponsorship covers individuals, teams or clubs, sports and events. It is now very rare to find any aspect of sport where there is not some form of sponsorship.

- **Individuals**   It is not just those who take part in individual sports (such as tennis and golf) who are sponsored. It is increasingly common for individuals within a team (i.e. soccer, rugby and basketball players) to have their own sponsorship, while the team as a whole may be separately sponsored as well. Most professional sportspeople are sponsored, often by more than one company. For example, a racing driver's overalls and car are often completely covered with sponsors' names and products. Each sponsor must pay for that space. If the sportsperson is particularly successful they can be paid very large amounts of money and have companies queueing up to sign them. It can reach the stage for some that they make far more out of sponsorship than they do from the actual sport in terms of prize money or wages.

- **Teams and clubs**   At just about any level, from small local soccer teams to full international teams, there is a great deal of sponsorship. Particularly successful teams can attract very large amounts, running into millions of pounds, which can have great benefits. Sometimes local firms or businesses sponsor local teams – this can be as basic as donating the match ball. This is a good system, as the local teams would not be able to attract major sponsors and small firms or businesses would not be able to spend sufficient money on very big clubs.

- **Sports**   Sometimes the actual sport itself, or its controlling association, is sponsored. This means that all the members of the association, including all the clubs and players, benefit. Many sports with a good image are chosen by sponsors and they are happy to help the sport nationally, not just in one area.

- **Events**   Events have become very popular with sponsors because they are certain to be associated with success and successful teams. Sponsors do not have to take the risk that an individual, or team, might fail. If they take charge of the whole event, and as long as the event or

Winning an Olympic gold medal in any of the major sporting activities just about guarantees the winner enough sponsorship deals to become a millionaire.

The sport of tennis has specific rules about the number, and size, of advertising logos which tennis players can wear on their clothing.

competition goes smoothly, they are guaranteed a lot of free advertising and publicity. All sorts of events are sponsored, from local gymnastic competitions right through to major international events such as the Olympic Games. In the case of the Olympics, the event is so big that it can attract a large number of sponsors, usually multi-national companies who want world-wide publicity for their products. Most big events are guaranteed to be a financial success because of the sponsors alone, whereas in the past they had to rely on making money from the number of people attending.

Types of sponsorship

Sponsorship can take many forms. It originally started in the days when there was more amateur sport (see page 79). It was a way of helping a sportsperson without directly giving them money, as this was not allowed. Now it takes the following forms:

- **Equipment**   As part of a sponsorship arrangement, a sportsperson is given all their equipment for their chosen sport. This equipment is manufactured by the sponsors and can range from sports shoes to rackets, even to specialist training equipment. Many sportspeople require lots of different types and forms of equipment so they can negotiate quite a lot of deals!

- **Clothing**   As well as the actual clothing worn by the sportsperson when taking part. This often includes other items to wear such as sun visors or baseball caps with the manufacturer's name on. There are often rules about how many, and where, these names can appear but the manufacturers make sure that theirs is clearly showing. Also, it is not only the brand names which appear – any part of the clothing is often used as 'advertising space' for anything from sports goods manufacturers to holiday resorts!

- **Accessories**   Some firms are prepared to pay for their product to be worn even though they have no direct link to the sport. This is why so many tennis players are sponsored to wear certain watches when they play (which can be seen on television as the player serves) and cricketers are paid to wear sunglasses.

- **Transport and travel**   This is often at least paid for and, in some cases, it is even provided. Car firms will provide free cars, often with drivers, for competitions and air travel companies will provide free flights. Even at lower levels, coach firms will provide free transport (or at least at a reduced cost) and local garages will provide cars and/or petrol.

- **Money**   Actual payments of money are made and the person sponsored can choose what to spend it on. If all the other aspects are covered then this just becomes an extra income for the sportsperson.

- **Training**   This can be sponsored in several ways. The facilities can be provided, or paid for, or paid time off work can be arranged to enable training to take place. In some sports, such as tennis, personal trainers or coaches are provided for individual players.

Many sports have their own award schemes sponsored by large companies.

Many events have their names changed each time they take place depending on who the sponsors are. What started off as the Football League Cup had various names until it became the Worthington Cup. The chances are that it might change its name again!

Australian bowler, Shane Warne, was paid to wear a Nike emblem earring whilst playing!

- **Entry fees and expenses**   These can mount up and be quite expensive and if not paid for could put a performer off taking part in a competition.
- **Food**   This is another very common form of sponsorship. There are many examples of butchers sponsoring field athletes who need a large protein input which they get from eating meat.

Benefits for sponsors

Sponsors will assist sport mainly because they get something out of it and it is worth their while to do so. These are the main benefits they can enjoy:

- **advertising** – this is undoubtedly the main reason why most sponsors get involved with sport. Sponsoring in any of the ways outlined in the last two pages is one of the most effective ways of advertising a product or service. It can also work out cheaper than many other forms of advertising, such as television, newspapers, billboards or radio. It also has the added advantage that if the event, or performer, is shown on television they get this extra publicity as a bonus. Some products are not allowed to be advertised on television (e.g. cigarettes and other tobacco products) so sponsorship can be a way around these rules by getting the companies and brand names shown on the television
- **tax relief** – big companies pay huge amounts of tax to the government and through sponsoring they can claim back some of this against the taxes they have to pay. This means that it can actually save them money to sponsor certain things
- **image** – sport can generate a good image as it can show a healthy, successful lifestyle. It is good for companies and products to be associated with this image – and particularly with individuals who have a good public image
- **research and development** – by getting performers to use their products, many sponsors are able to try out new developments in materials or equipment to see how well they work
- **goodwill** – although this is closely linked with image, many sponsors are prepared to help as a gesture of goodwill without any guarantee that they will gain from it, other than establishing a good public image
- **improved sales** – this is the main aim the companies have. They want more people to buy their products either because they have been used successfully or associated with a successful performance or event.

Throughout the Wimbledon Tennis Championships fortnight all of the players are collected from their hotels and driven back to them by a fleet of cars organized by sponsors.

There has been controversy for many years about the fact that tobacco companies manage to advertise their products by sponsoring sporting events. There are laws being introduced to try to stop this happening.

Advantages and disadvantages of sponsorship

Advantages	Disadvantages
Young and promising sportspeople are able to concentrate on their sport without many of the financial worries	The sport can lose its own identity and be dictated to by the sponsors. This can happen in the following ways:
Sports can be promoted and encouraged so that participation levels increase	Rules can be changed at the sponsor's request. This is particularly so in the case of what is appropriate to wear and sometimes the length of time the event is to last
The image of the sport can be improved with a good link up to a company which has a good image	The timing of events is often dictated by the sponsors, particularly when the sport is being televised. Times are chosen to suit an international audience and this might not be in the best interest of the performer or the sport
More money is provided for the sport to pay for administration, facilities, coaching, training and improving standards	Less successful sports and performers do not receive any sponsorship – or very little!
Bigger and better events can be staged and organized	A bad public image can damage a sport and reduce interest and participation
Award schemes can be paid for and advertised	If the sponsor has to withdraw, the sport or performer may not be able to carry on
Sponsors can get all of the benefits listed opposite	The sport may become over commercialized reducing the fun aspect of taking part
Competitions and leagues can be run, and prizes and money provided	Clothing may be changed to fit in with the sponsor's demands
Minority sports can be encouraged and financed	Specific dates of events may be dictated by the sponsors

QUESTIONS

1   Describe the range of sponsorship which exists in sport today including what and who may be sponsored.
2   Describe and explain what different forms of sponsorship exist for both sports performers and for specific sports.
3   What are the main advantages to a sport, or sportsperson of being sponsored?
4   What are the main benefits to the sponsors of sponsoring sport?
5   How easy might it be for either a sport or an individual to obtain sponsorship? What factors will influence this?
6   Explain and describe some of the main advantages and disadvantages associated with sponsorship in sport.

(b)   Media

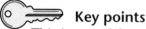 **Key points**

This is one of the most influential factors in local and national sport and is also rapidly changing. Although the main issues concerning the media are covered here, you will need to keep up to date with current events by making use of the various forms of the media.

Forms of media

The media consists of the following:

- **television** (terrestrial, cable, satellite and digital)
- **radio** (local and national)
- **the press** (newspapers, magazines, etc.)
- **books** (textbooks, autobiographies, etc.)
- **information and communications technology** (CD-ROMs, the Internet, DVDs, etc.)

Television

In the UK sport has been regulated and controlled since the Television Act 1954. This gave the Government power to draw up a list of protected events or 'listed events'. These cannot be shown exclusively on 'pay-per-view' channels (i.e. cable and satellite where you have to pay extra for some of the channels provided).

These listed events have had to be revised several times in recent years, mainly due to the very rapid change and development in the ways that television channels are now provided. In January 1999 they were revised into two groups. The main difference between the two is a legal requirement that Group A events must be made available to 'free-to-air' terrestrial television, and Group B events can have live coverage on pay TV, as long as there are satisfactory arrangements for secondary coverage (such as delayed coverage or edited highlights) by a free-to-air broadcaster.

The reasons for establishing and amending these lists was to make sure that the pay-per-view TV companies were not able to buy up all the rights to show all the major sporting events. The body which regulates the arrangements for the televising of sport is the Independent Television Commission (ITC).

Terrestrial television

Terrestrial television programmes are those which can be received by an ordinary television using an aerial. You must pay a licence fee to watch these programmes.

The following networks transmit throughout the UK:

- BBC1
- BBC2
- ITV (broken down into geographic regions)
- Channel 4
- Channel 5.

Sky Television 'bought' all the rights to show live coverage of the 1999 Ryder Cup and the BBC were allowed to show delayed coverage highlights in the evening.

Both the BBC channels receive funding from the Government to pay for making and transmitting programmes through the licence fee money which each household with a television must pay.

The other three channels are what is known as 'independent networks' and they raise all their money through advertising revenue for adverts shown during commercial breaks. These networks are also able to negotiate specific sponsorship deals with companies to have programmes with paid sponsorship.

Televised sport is one of the most popular areas of broadcasting. The sporting events which are shown on television are bid for by the television companies. This means that they have to negotiate with the individual sports (and sometimes it is with organizers of specific competitions) to have the right to televise that activity. This has lead to a lot of competition between the TV companies for the rights to show certain sports and the sports have been able to sell to the highest bidder.

Pay-per-view channels
Sky launched its Sky Sports service on the Astra satellite in 1991 which you could obtain by subscription in 1992. In August 1994, a second Sky Sports Channel was launched to be followed by a third one in 1996. In addition to this, there is a Eurosport Channel which is also available on satellite TV.

Television and sponsorship
The relationship between TV and sponsorship can be a very complex and controversial one. In 1994, a Government committee recommended that the BBC should stop broadcasting any sporting events sponsored by tobacco companies. The ITV network had stopped this in 1987 and even has its own code of practice which clearly lays out what is – and what is not – acceptable sponsorship.

This code lists prohibited sponsors (such as tobacco firms, betting companies etc.) and also sets the rules for how programmes themselves may be sponsored, including categories of presenters who may have certain restrictions placed upon them.

Types of programmes broadcast
There is a wide variety televised sports coverage including:

- live sporting action
- highlights programmes
- documentaries
- quiz programmes
- news bulletins
- information services (Ceefax and Teletext)
- coverage of major sporting events
- sporting magazine programmes
- education, schools programmes
- dedicated channels (such as Manchester United TV).

One of the reasons for the large and varied amount of sports coverage is that it is relatively cheap to televise. Many other programmes are far more expensive to produce – and do not have the uncertainty and drama of a live sports event.

Benefits TV brings to sport

Television clearly benefits from showing sport but it is not entirely a one-way process. Sport benefits, too, through:

- **increased popularity** – due to TV coverage many minority sports have greatly increased in popularity, and in their number of participants. For example, gymnastics nearly always has a boom period immediately following an Olympic Games where there has been extensive coverage
- **increased revenue** – through sponsorship and endorsements
- **direct payments** – from television for the rights to broadcast events.

Negative effects of media coverage on sport

For the most part involvement with the media brings benefits to sport but sometimes there are problems:

- television may intrude upon an event with cameras and crews, commentator's positions, etc.
- sometimes rules are changed or adapted to make sports more appealing to TV audiences
- timings can be dictated by the TV companies
- use of replays in slow motion and from various angles can undermine some officials' decisions
- if particular sports are not shown or featured they may decline in popularity
- some minor sports may lack coverage and find it hard to gain funding through sponsorship
- if matches/events are shown on TV it can discourage spectators from going to them; also it may clash with another live event and reduce attendance at that
- the media can intrude upon someone's privacy
- some aspects of a sport can be over-sensationalized in order to sell or promote a product/newspaper, etc.

Information and communications technology

This is an area which has increased very rapidly and only comparatively recently. The rise in the number of computers, in schools, at work and in the home, has opened up new possibilities for people.

CD-ROMs can be used as information sources or even as interactive programmes.

The Internet allows access to literally thousands of web sites throughout the world where you can get sports information on anything from aerobics to yachting.

Clubs and organizations are establishing their own web sites and it is now possible to find out about events and book tickets in advance using the Internet.

Radio

Most radio stations cover sport in much the same way as television. The obvious disadvantage is that they cannot broadcast pictures. However, because of this they are not regarded as rivals by TV and, particularly, satellite companies. They are therefore allowed to cover all the major sporting events. It

Snooker greatly increased in popularity when it was first televised and it was not shown until the start of colour transmission when people could see the colour of the balls!

The tie break was first introduced in tennis partly due to pressure from TV companies to make the game more appealing to TV audiences.

Information and communications technology has only been considered part of the media since the rapid increase and availability of home computers.

is quite common to have these events broadcast on TV at the same time as they are being transmitted by radio stations.

There are also specialist radio stations which concentrate on sports coverage, such as Radio 5 Live.

Radio has advantages over TV because:

- broadcasting costs are much lower as only one commentator is required (sometimes with an expert analyst) and the basic technology to transmit the broadcast
- radios are portable, cheap and plentiful (listeners can tune in while driving their cars). The potential audience is therefore bigger.

The press
This consists of newspapers and magazines. They cover sport in various ways and can be very influential:

- **newspapers** – all daily newspapers have sports sections. Some, such as the Sunday editions, have separate sports supplements. These can affect public opinion greatly as they are not only informative in that they print results, match reports, team news, rule changes and fixtures, but they also comment on many major sporting issues – and especially about sporting personalities!
- **magazines** – there has been an increase in the number of specialist sports magazines in recent years. Most sports have at least one publication devoted to them. They concentrate on sporting issues or on health and fitness and often contain very detailed information.

Books
These range from novels with sporting themes to textbooks on sport – such as this publication! Some of the most controversial books recently have been sporting autobiographies.

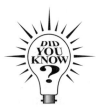

Two England soccer managers, Graham Taylor and Glenn Hoddle, lost their positions partly as a result of unfavourable media coverage – especially in the press!

QUESTIONS
1 Describe and explain what the media consists of.
2 What types of coverage does the media or television offer to viewers? Give examples of the different categories you have identified.
3 What positive effects can media coverage have on sport? Give examples to explain your answer.
4 What negative effects can the media have on sport? Give examples to explain your answer.

(c) Social and Cultural Aspects

 Key points

There are three key areas to this section:

- the way in which officials and players conduct themselves (including etiquette)
- the role of spectators (especially their behaviour)
- the differences between amateur and professional sport.

Officials and conduct

There are various types of officials (referees, judges, umpires etc.) depending on the activity. There are also different levels of officials (including minor ones such as linesman/referees, assistants, timekeepers, scorers etc.). All these people have to work together to make sure that the activity runs smoothly. Other responsibilities include interpreting the rules, laws or regulations of the activity, checking the equipment to be used, making sure the correct players are taking part, and timing the activity. Each physical activity has its own particular responsibilities.

Many sports, such as soccer, have 'retirement' ages for their officials and no matter how good they are, they are not allowed to continue beyond this age.

Whatever the differences, the qualities which officials must have are much the same and include:

- a full and thorough knowledge of the rules – decisions have to made during a game and the official in charge clearly needs to know them to maintain order
- a fair approach to the game – this means that they must be unbiased (or impartial) and not favour one team, or player, more than the other
- being in good physical condition – this can be as simple as having good eyesight or enough speed/stamina to keep up with the play
- being able to be firm and decisive – when in charge, officials must stop any arguments starting and their decision must be final.

The conduct of players

Etiquette is a conventional rule or form of behaviour as opposed to an enforceable rule, law or regulation. In all activities, there is acceptable etiquette but it is not written down in any rule book and it is up to the participants to behave in the correct way. Some examples of correct etiquette include:

Most sports have players' associations that deal with their own players who do not observe good etiquette.

- **soccer** – if a player is injured, a player will kick the ball out of play to stop the game to allow treatment. On the re-start throw-in, the opposition will throw the ball back in to the opponents who stopped the game instead of their own players
- **tennis** – at the end of a match opponents shake hands and also thank and shake hands with the umpire
- **squash** – players will call their own fouls shots such as a 'double hit' or 'bump ball', especially if the marker could not detect them.

Role of spectators

It would be unthinkable for most sports to take place without spectators and many clubs rely on them. However, spectators can be both good and bad. The following are the ways spectators can affect sport:

- **Finance**   Spectators pay to come and watch matches/games and this can be a very large source of income. Big professional clubs can earn a lot of money from what is known as 'gate receipts', but these large crowds can also cause the clubs problems:
  - **facilities** must be provided for all the spectators including toilets, food and drink, separate family enclosures, 'home' and 'away' areas and even lighting and heating
  - **supervision and control** must be set up. There is a responsibility to make sure that all spectators are safe and well looked after. This means that the clubs must employ stewards and marshals and pay for the services of the police – often the police fee is one of the largest bills that the clubs have to pay!
- **Crowd influence**   It is generally thought to be an advantage for a team to play 'at home' as most supporters encourage and motivate their team. Many players find it very intimidating to play 'away' knowing that the opposing fans will be very critical of them and of any mistakes they might make.
- **Behaviour**   There are many examples of incidents where the behaviour of the spectators has been totally unacceptable and disasters have happened. One of these was at the Heysell Stadium, when fighting broke out between Liverpool and Juventus supporters and Italian fans were crushed by a damaged stand.

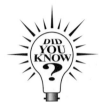

Many of the regulations which relate to stadiums and how crowds must be controlled came about as a direct result of the Hillsborough disaster and the report on it, known as the Taylor Report.

Amateur and professional sport

Professional sport is a relatively recent thing, especially in some sports such as athletics and rugby union. Sometimes it is very difficult to tell the difference between a professional and an amateur. These are the traditional definitions:

- **amateur** – someone who takes part in sport or activity as a pastime or hobby rather than for gain. They participate for enjoyment only, do not get paid and usually have a full time job
- **professional** – someone who takes part in a sport or an activity as a means of earning their living. They get paid for participating and do it as a full-time job.

Look at pages 70–3 to see how amateurs can 'bend' these rules and get financial support through sponsorship.

QUESTIONS

1 Name **three** different activities and describe who the officials would be for each of them. Explain the qualities these officials would need.

2 What is meant by etiquette? Give an example of it from a sporting activity.

3 Describe **three** different ways that spectators can have an effect upon sport.

4 Explain and describe the differences between amateur and professional sport.

(d) Influences of Local and National Providers

Key points

You will need to know how provision is made for sport – in other words, how and why sporting opportunities including funding are made available. There is a very close link between this section and the one on facilities on pages 92–3.

Local provision

A great deal of sport is organized at a local level and the way it is run will vary from region to region. Many areas have sports development officers who work closely with schools and clubs to promote sport. Some of these will have links to specific sports, such as netball or rugby, and others will deal with sport in general.

Local provision usually falls in one of two categories:

- **public facilities** – such as sports/leisure centres, provided by local authorities
- **private facilities** – such as sports/fitness clubs which are privately owned and run.

These are dealt with in more detail on pages 90–3.

Sports clubs

At all levels of sport, the main providers are clubs, all with much the same structure and organization. They all have:

- a **chairperson** – in overall control of meetings, etc.
- a **vice-chair** – who deputizes for the chairperson when necessary
- a **secretary** – who deals with all the administration, writing and answering letters, taking minutes of meetings, etc.
- a **treasurer** – in charge of financial matters, paying bills, match fees, etc.
- **committee members** – elected by members to have regular meetings to make decisions on behalf of the club
- **members** – everyone who belongs to the club.

Many clubs have very strong links with schools. This is because young people often first take up a sport at school where they are introduced to it and learn the basics. They may then want to progress further, and clubs are keen to attract new members – especially young ones!

Funding of sport

The financing, or funding, of sport is necessary so that we can have facilities, provision of various activities and efficient organization. The most costly of these are the facilities – see pages 92–3. How the money is raised or provided includes :

- **Clubs**   They are able to raise funds through membership fees, fund raising such as sponsored events or car boot sales and also through grants from local authorities or even sports governing bodies.

In the largest professionally-run clubs, some of the officials, such as the secretary and treasurer are full-time paid officials. In most smaller clubs, they just do it to keep the club going and work for free!

Nearly all clubs have junior sections which are organized especially for the young players/ performers. They also usually run specific junior teams and/or tournaments.

- **Charities** many sports associations are registered as charities and this can gain them exemption from paying taxes. They do not have to make a profit so they can re-invest all of their own money.

- **Professional clubs** Many sports have professional clubs which are run as businesses and have to raise all their own finance. They raise this money through spectators paying to watch matches, and merchandising, where they make money through the sale of goods associated with the club.

- **Governing bodies** These receive money and can also raise money, sometimes by running tournaments. The Wimbledon Tennis Championships, for example, raise millions of pounds each year which is then distributed amongst tennis clubs and used for the good of the sport.

- **National and local government** A great deal of money is raised each year through national and local taxes which all adults must pay. Some of this money goes to sport to help with the funding of facilities and running them. Much of this money is also available through grants which sporting bodies must make applications for.

- **Sponsorship** Vast amounts of money are provided for sport each year through sponsorship deals. See pages 71–3 where this was covered in detail.

- **Gambling** Some sports have specific links with gambling: football has the pools companies and horseracing has betting agencies. Since 1994 the National Lottery has provided millions of pounds which sport has benefited from and Sport England (formerly the Sports Council) is responsible for the allocation of National Lottery funds to sporting organizations.

- **The media** Many sports bodies deal directly through the media to negotiate fees and they will pay to be allowed to cover their sport. With the large amount of television coverage now there is even money available for the smaller sports.

Manchester United Football Club is one of the world's most successful professional clubs. In 1999 they had an annual income in excess of £90 million!

QUESTIONS

1 Describe how sport is organized at a local level. Explain the links which might exist between schools and clubs.

2 Describe how sports clubs are organized. Name some of the officials and describe briefly what their roles are.

3 Describe some of the ways in which sport is funded. What help does the National Lottery provide?

(e) International Sport

 Key points

You need to know what international sport consists of and the political and financial issues associated with staging events. Also, the various problems which have occurred at them. You might also be asked to give details about some of the Olympic Games.

The Olympic Games

These were re-started in 1896 by Baron Pierre de Coubertin, based on the Ancient Greeks' Olympic Games. These are the specific Games you need to have knowledge of:

- **1936, Berlin** – these Games were used as a propaganda exercise by Adolph Hitler who was ruling Germany as the head of the Nazi party. He tried to use the Games to promote his ideas about the Germans being the master race and that the Jews and other ethnic groups should be persecuted. His plan backfired mainly due to the success of the black American athlete, Jesse Owens, who went on to win four gold medals and be the hero of the Games.

- **1968, Mexico City** – there was controversy when Mexico was awarded the Games because it is situated at a very high altitude. This was an advantage to the athletes who had trained in these conditions. Also Mexico was a very poor country and it was doubtful if they could afford to stage the event. During a medal ceremony, two black American athletes, Tommie Smith and John Carlos, gave a 'Black Power' salute with gloved hands to highlight the racial discrimination that existed in America – as a result they were sent home!

- **1972, Munich** – there was another Black Power protest at these Games by two Americans but the main controversy was the attack on some of the athletes. A group of Palestinian terrorists attacked members of the Israeli team. Eight terrorists beseiged the Israeli quarters, killed two of the team and took nine others hostage. After a gun siege, all of the hostages, five terrorists and one German police officer were killed. This established security as a major issue for future Games.

- **1976, Montreal** – South Africa had been banned from the Games since 1964 because of its apartheid policy (where black people were discriminated against). Because a New Zealand rugby team had toured South Africa, many other African nations threatened to boycott the Games if New Zealand were allowed to take part. Because they did, 30 African nations stayed away – the start of a long period of political boycotts for various reasons.

- **1980, Moscow** – the Soviet Union invaded Afghanistan in 1979 and still had a force there in 1980. Many countries demanded that the Soviet Union withdraw their forces or they would boycott the Games. As a result, a total of 52 nations boycotted them. The USA refused to let any competitors attend but the British government 'advised' its competitors against going. With many of the strongest countries not taking part, it was felt that the Games were devalued.

- **1984, Los Angeles** – The organizers could not help following a Soviet-hosted Games with an American one and the Soviet Union took the opportunity to 'get their own back' and boycott these Games! The official reason was 'concern over security arrangements'. Another excuse was that the Games were becoming over commercialized which the Communist countries objected to – in total 15 countries boycotted, all of them Communist ones, including the Soviet Union.

- **1988, Seoul** – Seoul is in South Korea and there had been a long-standing dispute between them and their Communist neighbours, North Korea. There were real worries and great tension up until the Games because of this, especially as the North Koreans had demanded that they be allowed to host some of the events. Although there was a boycott by five countries (including North Korea) there was little great controversy. The main problem was the start of drug scandals when Ben Johnson, who won the 100 metres, was disqualified for failing a drug test.

- **1992, Barcelona** – these were comparatively incident-free. There were a lot of new faces following the break-up of the eastern European Communist countries and South Africa was re-admitted after finally scrapping its apartheid policy. There was some more drug controversy with various performers failing drug tests and being sent home.

The Los Angeles Games were the first ones to run at a financial profit although it had to be called a 'surplus' because of the rules at that time. This was due to massive sponsorship deals and it changed cities views about hosting the Games – from now on they all wanted to!

Advantages and disadvantages of staging international events

There are a great many international events which are now held regularly, including the Commonwealth Games, Pan American Games, Wimbledon and World Championships in athletics, rugby, cricket and soccer. All of these demand a lot of attention and are very popular.

The advantages include:

- raising the profile and image of the hosts
- creating more wealth and money through attendance, tourism, sponsorship etc.
- creating more and better facilities for the hosts
- raising the profile of sport and sporting success in the host country.

The disadvantages include:

- running at a loss if expenses exceed the profits
- 'international incidents' disrupting the competition, such as boycotts, etc.
- security implications and responsibilities and the cost involved
- failing to cope with the demands in terms of media provision or facility provision.

QUESTIONS

1 Describe the controversial issues surrounding **three** different Olympic Games held since 1936.

2 Describe and explain the advantages to be gained from hosting a major international sporting event.

3 Describe and explain the disadvantages of hosting a major international sporting event.

8 Factors Affecting Individual Participation

(a) School

Key points

Remember that all the topics in this section refer specifically to *individual participation* and this is the important link between all of the topics. Schools and their influence should be considered as an important factor influencing young people to take part in sport.

Role of the school

In 1988 the Education Reform Act stated that PE was to be taught in schools in England and Wales. In 1992 the details of what should be taught as Physical Education were made law in the National Curriculum. All National Curriculum subjects taught in schools are governed by guidelines so that all pupils are taught a similar and balanced programme.

The reasons why schools make the provision for PE include:

- it is a legal requirement
- it provides a balance in the teaching programme as it is a practical subject that contrasts with classroom-based activities
- it improves health and fitness levels
- it reflects the importance of sport and physical activity in society
- it prepares young people to take part in sporting activity on leaving school.

Schools also have different ways in which they make this PE provision. These include:

- **timetabled PE lessons** – known as 'core time' lessons because they take place in time allocated to this subject area
- **extra curricular activities** – these usually take place after school or at lunchtimes
- **clubs and team practice sessions** – these may be specifically arranged for the school teams or just as clubs where different activities are available or there is an opportunity to have more practice of activities already covered in core time
- **examination-based courses** – such as GCSE Physical Education. These will usually be extra timetabled lessons in addition to PE, which is provided for everyone in core time
- **sports performance awards** – most physical activities have their own associated award schemes (such as athletics, gymnastics and swimming)
- **outside visits** – to leisure centres, fitness gyms, etc.

There used to be only two things which schools had to provide for their pupils by law – these were religious education and physical education!

Research has shown that once they have left school, many young people do not take part in any organized physical activity at all! This is despite the health benefits you gain from taking part.

- **links with local sports clubs** – see page 80 for details of this. They are usually very firmly established
- **cross-curricular links with other subject areas** – for example, diet might be studied in food technology, or many health-related fitness topics in science lessons
- **introducing new sports, providing equipment and facilities** – many activities have very specialized and expensive equipment which young people might not have access to outside school.

Obviously, the skills and expertise of the staff will also be important. Only qualified people are allowed to teach PE and they may have different interests and specialist strengths which they like to concentrate on. A positive attitude and approach from PE teachers can have a marked effect and a bad experience in PE can put someone off it for life. School is probably the first place where anyone plays properly organized sport and takes part in matches against other opponents.

The role of the teacher

A teacher is usually the person who first introduces young people to physical activities. Pupils may not have participated before. By way of introduction, basic skills, rules and techniques are taught at this stage.

Most children start school between the ages of four and five and experience up to six areas of activity. They do not take part in the same way as they will from the age of eleven upwards but instead do very basic introductory work, to prepare them for the more complex work later.

The following are the six areas of activity which pupils can take at school:

- **Athletic activities**
- **Dance**
- **Games** – usually divided into invasion games, net/wall games and striking/fielding/target games
- **Gymnastics** – including trampoline
- **Swimming and water safety**
- **Outdoor education and adventurous activities.**

There are no specialist PE teachers at primary and junior school. They only start to teach pupils from Key Stage 3 onwards – which is from the age of eleven upwards

QUESTIONS

1 Explain the reasons why schools provide Physical Education as part of their curriculum, or school programme.

2 Describe, and explain, the ways in which schools make provision for Physical Education.

3 Explain the role and influence of teachers in encouraging young people to take part in regular Physical Education.

4 Explain how school can encourage individual participation in sport.

(b) Changing Attitudes

 Key points

Although this section is concerned with changing attitudes it also links in to how these changing attitudes can lead to either an increase, or a decrease, in individual participation.

Attitudes of society

The attitude of society may change over a period of time and be influenced by a variety of factors. Society may view an activity as desirable, beneficial or even just enjoyable, and for these reasons the amount of participation in them may increase. Examples of this include:

- **Jogging** – over the last ten years there has been a tremendous increase in the number of jogging clubs which have started up. Many of them have members who wish to take part in events such as the London marathon. The London race is always oversubscribed with more runners wanting to run than there are places available. This is partly due to the fact that society views this activity as a healthy and worthwhile one and the high level of media coverage has helped this image.
- **Organized women's activities** – until recently there were very many activities that were considered to be 'unsuitable' for women to take part in. This included many of the long distance races and even activities such as the triple jump. The growth of women's sport has partly come about due to society changing its attitude. It has now accepted that women can take part in activities such as rugby, soccer and cricket just as well, and successfully, as men.
- **Any activity enjoying international success or high media coverage** – if activities are performed successfully and featured regularly in the media they are likely to change societies attitude in favour of them.

On the other hand, society may have an attitude towards an activity which it considers unsuitable for some reason. Examples of this include:

- **Boxing** – medical opinion has influenced public opinion that boxing is an unsuitable sport due to the damage that can be inflicted on boxers. There have been some deaths of boxers and many examples of serious injuries as a result of punches or through the long-term effects of receiving them. Calls for the sport to be banned, demonstrations against contests taking place and mounting medical evidence have led to decreasing numbers of clubs in some places.
- **Bad publicity may put off participants** – the high level of positive drug tests in some sports such as weightlifting and athletics may have the effect of turning society against them. It is also likely to influence parents against encouraging their children to become involved.

There is a world-wide increase in the membership of gymnastic clubs every four years following its media coverage at the Olympics.

Disabled athletes

Disabled people have not always been given the consideration, help and encouragement that they are today. This is part of a changing attitude by society in general, making sure that equal rights and equal opportunities are afforded to disabled people in all walks of life. Examples of this include:

- sports organizations now have disabled sections which cater specifically for the disabled participants. This can mean sorting out adapted rules, regulations, playing areas and equipment to allow all to take part
- facilities must by law consider the disabled in terms of access (wheelchair ramps, automatic doors, lifts etc.), parking (allocated disabled bays close to the building) and facilities (disabled toilets and changing facilities).

It is a requirement that, immediately following an Olympic Games, the host city must hold the Para-Olympics for all disabled competitors.

The effects of agencies

Agencies are organizations which in some way have an influence on sport and/or participation. In the UK one of the most important ones is Sport England (the new name of the former Sports Council). It has three specific aims:

- to increase the number of people involved in sport
- to encourage the provision of more places to play sport
- to give more medals through higher standards of performance in sport.

Obviously, promoting these aims can only change attitudes in favour of greater participation in sport. When the Sports Council was in existence, the first of its specific aims was, 'To increase participation in sport and physical recreation'. It attempted to do this in the following ways:

- awarding regional participation grants to local organizations
- running campaigns such as 'Sport for All', 'Ever Thought of Sport?', 'What's Your Sport?'
- funding development staff to help governing bodies of sport
- organizing programmes to promote sport through other agencies.

Sport England intends to continue with these aims and initiatives.

QUESTIONS

1 Explain how attitudes to sport may have changed in recent years.
2 Describe, giving examples, how attitudes have changed to make some sports more popular than they were.
3 Describe, giving examples, how attitudes have changed making some sporting activities more unpopular in terms of the number of people participating in them.
4 What roles can, and do, some of the sporting agencies play in increasing participation in sport?

(c) Social Groupings

 Key points

Any grouping such as a peer group, family, a person's gender or race can influence how much someone participates in sport. The influence may be positive or negative. In some cases the influence may be one that the individual cannot respond to, for example, if they cannot afford to take up an activity.

Peer group

Your peers are people who are of the same age and status as you. To most young people, this would be the group of friends, probably from school, whom they mix with most.

Peers are considered to be one of the most powerful influences on any person and 'peer pressure' (being encouraged to go along with what others are doing) can be very powerful. It can have the following effects on your attitude to sport:

- If your peers are very much in favour of sport and physical activity it is very likely that you will feel encouraged to join in with them. Most of your school PE will be with your peers. They will be team-mates, partners and opponents so this can have a very positive effect.
- If your peers are anti-sport it can have completely the opposite effect. They may encourage you not to take part in PE lessons, and certainly not to get involved in activities and teams out of school time. There may even be encouragement to lead an unhealthy lifestyle in terms of smoking, alcohol and even drug abuse. So the effect can be a very negative one.

It is very difficult for an individual to go against a majority group and it is for this reason that peer group influence is so powerful and an important factor to consider.

Family

The attitude of family, and especially parents, is also very important. If parents are very much in favour of the benefits of sport, they will almost certainly pass this attitude on to their children. There are many cases where children of quite famous sports performers have followed their parents' examples and played sport at a high level. Parents can help and encourage in the following ways:

- **by providing equipment** – for many sports certain equipment is essential to enable you to play. It may also, be expensive and need a financial commitment
- **by providing transport** – one of the major problems for young people is that they are not able to transport themselves. This usually means that it is left to parents to find the time and the means.

Not all parents take a positive attitude to sports activities. Some may even discourage taking part which will clearly have a bad effect on the young people.

Gender

On page 86, you can see that attitudes of society have changed towards women participating in sport. However there is still a certain amount of sexual discrimination against women as the following shows:

- **fewer events** – many events are held for men only and in many professional sports there are no organized women's events
- **less prize money** – nearly all events have less prize money for women than for men
- **lower profile** – women's events are not so well promoted or publicised
- **women are banned** – in the contact sports such as soccer and rugby, women are not allowed to compete against men so this can reduce their opportunities.

Race

The most significant example of race being a factor affecting sports participation is that of the apartheid laws in South Africa. Until they were ended in 1994, under these rules black and Asian people were segregated and treated as 'second class citizens'. They had very few rights, opportunities or facilities. This meant that people who were not white had totally separate schools, cinemas, living areas and even transport. Sports facilities were also separate, which meant that black and Asian people were only allowed very limited sporting opportunities.

Racial discrimination has also existed in other countries, especially the USA. It is an issue which is being addressed by many countries.

Socio-economic factors

This concerns people who find it difficult to afford to take part in sport and are therefore influenced against it for purely financial reasons. It is not only in poor countries that people experience problems. In the UK there are people who cannot afford to take part in sport – especially those activities where the costs of buying equipment, hiring facilities, travelling, etc. may be high.

One of the main reasons apartheid was abolished was because of the world-wide ban on sporting links with South Africa until they changed their laws.

QUESTIONS

1 What do you understand by the term 'peers'? How can peer group pressure affect an individual participating in sport?

2 What influence can family, and particularly parents, have on individuals participating in sport?

3 What effects may gender, race and socio-economic status have on participation?

(d) Leisure Time

Definition
Leisure time is when you are free to choose to do what you choose. To many people this is after work or school. However, not all of this is really free time because there are various essential activities that you must fit in, such as sleeping, eating and household chores. You may also need to spend some time travelling.

Key points
You should have an understanding of:

- what leisure time is
- the reasons for an increase in its availability
- how various bodies and organizations provide for people to participate in sporting activities during their leisure time.

Reasons for increased leisure time
It is important to know that leisure time has been increasing. There are many reasons for this including:

- **greater automation at home and work** – there are many more machines capable of doing jobs which used to take a long time. Labour-saving devices (i.e. automatic washing machines) leave individuals with more spare time. In the workplace, the rapid developments in technology, mainly computers, has also reduced many workloads
- **shorter working week** – the average working week is now considerably less than it was even ten years ago. This leaves people with more time
- **part-time work** – many people are opting to work part-time rather than full time, especially if someone else in a household already has a full-time job
- **unemployment levels** – unfortunately, there are quite high unemployment levels, particularly in some areas, and this means that people have more time on their hands even though this is not by choice.

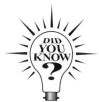

The leisure industry is considered to be one of the fastest growing and most important industries in the UK today.

Leisure provision
Due to the increase in available leisure time there has also been a need to provide more leisure services. Much of the leisure provision is made by local authorities (see page 80) whose responsibility it is to do so. This can range from providing a library or allotments, right through to swimming pools or sports halls. Most local authorities provide a leisure centre in their area, usually designed to cater for as many activities as possible.

It is not just local authorities who provide leisure facilities. There are private companies who do so as well. Cinemas, bowling alleys, discos and clubs are privately run and aim to make money out of the leisure needs of their customers.

Provision – needs and range

One of the challenges in providing for leisure is the variety of people who have to be catered for in terms of age, ability and interest. There is quite a large range of identified 'user groups' and these include:

- **Mothers and young children** – this is an increasing user group. It has a difficult demand as often young children have to be looked after while mothers take part in physical activity. There really has to be a double provision.
- **Retirement age groups** – with many people taking early retirement, this can start from the age of 50. This provision must take into account the effects of the ageing process, making sure that the activities are suitable for a range of ages.
- **Unemployed groups** – there may be a wide age range within these groups. They may also want access to facilities during the day when other people are working.

To cater for all of these groups, the provision has to be very varied and flexible and the timings of the various programmes has to be considered carefully.

Another consideration is the ability of the user groups to pay to use the facilities. Many local authority run facilities offer reduced rates for the unemployed so they are not prevented from participating because they cannot afford to do so.

Role of Sport England

The sports organizations such as Sport England (formerly the Sports Council) have made it a priority to both identify, and make provision for, various user groups. Page 87 looked at the roles of these agencies in changing attitudes. One of their specific aims is to increase the use of facilities by:

- encouraging new and improved facilities
- researching and preparing designs for sports buildings and systems
- designing, building and testing innovative facilities and systems such as artificial pitches
- identifying good practice of design, facilities or management
- funding research into sports requirements.

QUESTIONS

1 Describe **three** possible reasons why there may now be increased available leisure time.

2 What sort of provisions are made for more leisure time?

3 State, and describe **three** different 'user groups' and explain what sort of provision might be appropriate for each.

4 What role do sports organizations such as Sport England play in helping cater for increased participation during leisure time?

(e) Facilities Available

 Key points

This section considers:

- what sorts of facilities exist
- where they are located and why
- who is likely to use them
- the variety of people, and interests, which have to be catered for.

Again, these must be considered as factors which can affect individual participation.

Location of facilities

Sports facilities vary considerably but fall into two main categories:

- **Outdoor facilities** – including sports pitches, water sports areas, outdoor pursuit areas and any natural features which might be used for sporting events such as cross-country courses.
- **Indoor facilities** – these are usually specifically built for certain sports (such as swimming pools, fitness gyms), or built to be flexible to allow a variety of sports (sports halls or leisure centres).

The main difference between indoor and outdoor facilities is that there is usually more choice of where you can locate indoor ones. The factors to consider regarding location include:

- **population and expected use** – there is no point providing a facility if there is no one around to use it. Because of this most of the major indoor facilities are built in areas with a large population
- **access** – people need to be able to reach the facility easily. They may travel there by road, rail or even aeroplane. (This might be important if you were hoping to hold major international events in the facility.) All the transport links need to be considered and either provided or improved
- **parking** – for many local facilities, the most common way of getting there is to drive. Suitable and adequate parking space is therefore necessary
- **cost** – this is not always just the cost of building the facility, but also the cost of the site to build it on. The building costs will be much the same wherever it is. However, the price of land can vary considerably and this can be the main constraint over location
- **natural features** – such things as good drainage or climate may be very important when considering where to build stadiums
- **demand** – the facility may be intended for a particular activity and you would have to check if there was enough demand in the particular area to justify locating the facility there
- **competition and rival facilities** – there is little point in duplicating a facility if one already exists, unless the demand is so great that one facility cannot satisfy it. Several sports halls in an area might all be well used, but it is unlikely that including a swimming pool or ice rink with each of them would be worthwhile

Many professional football clubs have sold off their old grounds which were situated close to city and town centres and built new ones on the outskirts of the towns. This makes for easier access and cheaper costs!

- **flexibility and versatility** – it is an advantage if the facility can be used for a variety of things. Some activities become trends and if the interest drops, and that is all the facility can be used for, it causes problems. That is why so many leisure centres are the main provision, because they are flexible in what they can put on and provide
- **dual use** – many school sites are dual use so that facilities are not duplicated in the area. This means that the school has use of the facilities during the school day with other user groups in the community there during the evenings, weekends and school holidays. Therefore it may be worth updating or improving existing facilities rather than building brand new ones.

User groups

A variety of facilities has to be provided because there are many different groups wishing to use them. They will all have different needs and requirements including the following:

- **Individuals** – obviously this category will be huge, from the person who wants to book a badminton court to someone who wants to weight train
- **Teams** – this is also a large category, from cricket teams who want an indoor net area to squash teams who need courts provided
- **Clubs** – there is a wide range here, from sporting clubs through to social and recreational clubs who may just need an area to meet rather than specific equipment
- **Regional/national squads** – the requirements of these are more demanding. A higher standard of equipment may be required and there are centres of excellence to cater for this. At the highest level, specialist training areas are required, for example, in gymnastics where training 'pits' are needed, along with specialist coaches. These centres are also used to run competitions
- **Challenging activities** – these include the more demanding outdoor pursuits such as caving, rock climbing, etc. Facilities have to be provided for participants.

There is not a swimming pool in the UK which makes money because it is one of the most expensive facilities to run. This is because of the cost of maintenance, heating and treating the water and safely staffing it. It is also why there are no privately-run swimming pools.

QUESTIONS

1 What are the main types of indoor and outdoor sports facilities?

2 Explain and describe **three** main factors which must be taken into account when deciding where a sports facility should be located.

3 What special considerations might be taken into account when deciding the location of an outdoor facility?

4 Name **three** different user groups which must be catered for and describe briefly what their needs might include.

Advice on the Exam Questions

This section deals with general points about examination technique as well as looking at the types of questions you are likely to be asked. It also looks at how you should go about answering the questions which are included in this book.

Examination technique

These are some basic guidelines which you *must* consider because they can make a great difference to your ability to answer a question properly and correctly.

- The question paper is divided up into two sections. Section A: Health Related Fitness and Section B: Sport and Society. You need to be familiar with all of the topics covered in the eight sections of this book because there must be a question on each of the section areas in each year's exam paper.

- Read the question carefully! There is no additional reading time, just the two hours to answer the questions. Don't just pick out key words and start answering the question. Make sure that you are actually answering the question set, rather than the question you would have liked to have been set! There can be a temptation to write all that you know about a particular topic – such as sponsorship in sport – then, when you look closely at the question, it may just be about the advantages to an individual of being sponsored. So much of what you have written may be irrelevant and worth no marks at all!

- Check to see if any examples are asked for. Often questions are worded so that you have to explain or describe something and give examples. These examples are often the easiest part of the question and you may well be able to give them from your own experience. Unfortunately, they are often missed out! Look at page 87, questions 2 and 3. Both of these ask for a description with examples and you can see some basic, straightforward examples included in the text which you can give as part of your answer. If you did not give the examples here to further explain the answer, you would only obtain a maximum of half of the available marks for the question.

- Check all completed questions! Leave yourself some time at the end of the exam to check your answers, or better still, check each answer against the question set as soon as you have finished it. If you then realize you have not answered the question as set, you at least should have time to change it or add a new one. This problem should not arise if you have followed the first tip and really checked the question before starting it!

- Diagrams are allowed as part of your answer, and this is stated on the front of the examination paper. You might find that you can answer a question much more easily by drawing a diagram than you can in words. Look at page 34, question 3, 'Choose **five** different bones in the body and describe exactly where they are located'. If you drew a diagram of the body, with the bones in the correct place, and labelled them, you would get full marks if they were correct. This may be a far easier way for you to answer the question rather than to struggle with the correct words. Remember though, you must clearly label your diagram, and your diagram must be clear. Don't expect to be able to answer every question with a diagram – be selective!

- **Bold** words which appear like **this** in the exam question are the key words to the question. They are written in bold to draw your attention to them. You must make sure that your answer refers to these words and that you have taken advantage of the help the examiner has given you.

- Key words – you will see the same words appearing time and again in the questions you are asked. You must be aware of what they mean and how long your answer will need to be to match the key word used. These are the key words you are likely to see, and what they require of you:
  - *Give, state* or *name*: one word would be enough here. For example, to the question 'Give one component of fitness', the answer, 'Endurance' would be enough. You don't have to give more and you would probably be wasting your time if you did so. This applies equally if the word at the start of the question is 'state ' or 'name'.
  - *Explain, describe* or *consider*: these words mean that you will have to write a fairly long answer with much more detail. For example, the question 'Explain one component of fitness', would need a different approach from the first example above. Here you could still answer 'endurance' but you would have to go on to explain what endurance actually was. By the time you have considered local muscular endurance and cardiovascular endurance, and described the effect it has on the various body systems, together with ways it can be improved and tested, you will have written a long and quite complex answer! These types of questions are the ones which tend to appear at the end of each set of questions. They are what is known as 'differentiated'. They are usually worth the most marks, are the most complicated and difficult, and the ones you need to answer well to get a higher grade. They are also likely to be the ones you struggle with the most!

- Content and terminology – you must try to get used to the specialist terminology of the subject. This means that you need to know and understand the words which are used in the syllabus (and therefore the ones which are used in this book, as they match the syllabus) so that you are absolutely clear what they mean. For example, on page 64, there is reference to *somatotypes*, including *endomorphs, mesomorphs* and *ectomorphs*. These are not words you would use in everyday language but they are specialist terms for PE. Therefore you need to know and understand them as they will be used in exam questions. This is doubly important because if you don't know them you will not even be able to attempt the question, nor will you be able to include them in any answers you try to give. Using the correct terminology in an answer is always easier, and likely to get you more marks, than trying to describe something in your own words.

- Mark allocation – at the end of each question on the question paper there will be a number in brackets. This is the number of marks allocated to that particular question. The answer you give must be in line with the number of marks available for that question. If there is one mark it probably corresponds with one of the *give, state* or *name* key words explained above, and you may only have to give a one word, or very brief answer to get the mark available. More marks available means that more detail is required in your answer. Questions with higher marks match the *explain, describe* and *consider* key words, and you must answer accordingly. Look at question 1 on page 91: 'Describe **three** possible reasons why there may now be increased available leisure time'. If that question appeared on an examination paper it would probably have a mark allocation of six marks and you would be awarded two marks for each of the reasons you gave. It is also fairly likely that the word **three** would be in bold print to give you the full indication of what is expected of you. The simple rule is that more marks require more detailed answers and therefore longer answers.

Examination hints and tips

It would be a good idea to treat your actual examination like a practical session and approach it in the same way by doing the following:

- **Practise** Any skill you wish to develop you improve by practising. If you want to improve the skill of answering exam questions, practise them! Try to get hold of past papers, and mark schemes and just practise answering questions. To start with you can have the answers in front of you and just practise getting them into order and writing them down neatly and clearly. As you get better and more confident, answer the questions using the knowledge you have; check the relevant section of this book; read it; then select a question related to it and attempt an answer. The final stage is to go on to trying to attempt any answer on any aspect of the examination and check your results against the type of answer you should have given. The more you practise the better you will become!
- **Check the rules!** You wouldn't attempt to take part in any physical activity without knowing the rules first. Treat this exam the same way. All the help given in this section is basically laying out the rules of the examination. You are the participant and the marker is the referee who will judge how well you have interpreted the rules and how well you performed in terms of matching the task set.
- **Peaking** The day of the exam is when you want to be at your best. Plan ahead for it. Don't leave things too late and make sure you are ready to give your best on the day!
- **Warm up** Get yourself properly prepared physically and mentally for this exam and go in feeling as ready for it as you can. Your preparation is probably going to be over about two years and it all depends on a performance lasting two hours. What you actually achieve in that time is going to be vitally important.
- **Be competitive** Have a positive approach. The exam questions are not set as pitfalls and deliberately difficult. The question setter does want you to be able to answer the questions set and they should not be beyond your capability. If you have prepared yourself properly, think clearly and perform to the best of your ability, you should be able to do well and get the grade you deserve.